comfort ♡

CANDICE BROWN

Comfort

DELICIOUS BAKES & FAMILY TREATS

EBURY PRESS

Dedicated to Flo,
always x

INTRODUCTION 6

Cook's notes 18

A bake for every occasion 24

Cakes 28

Brownies, biscuits & traybakes 64

Tarts & pastries 90

Puddings & preserves 118

Savoury bakes, bites & soups 156

Breads & buns 212

Index 244

Conversion charts 252

Acknowledgements 254

My first book could only ever be about one thing – comfort.

Comfort foods, comfort baking... all those things you love to eat that make you feel warm and cozy inside. Much like the food I was brought up on and that my Mam and Nan cooked for my family. For me, food should be a celebration of all of the things that I – and others – love.

For my first 21 years, I lived in pubs that my parents ran. I would watch my Dad prepare meat – skinning rabbits, plucking pheasants – for my Mam, who'd use it to make rich, hearty pies. Our family dinners were so generous and comforting – there was always enough for seconds or thirds.

I think that certain dishes should bring back memories or trigger your senses; and they should make you smile. The earliest memories I have of baking are with my dear Nan – Margaret Florence Brown, my Dad's mum. She was the absolute apple of my eye and the most incredible woman. She also happened to be an amazing cook and baker. I spent a lot of time – nearly all my school holidays – with Nan and Grandad in Edmonton, where I was born, and I loved every second of it.

Nan used to make and bake everything from scratch. When she was in the kitchen I would drag one of the chairs through from the living room, put it right next to her and stand on it, so I could watch her while she made something delicious like her Bakewell tart or my Grandad's absolute favourite, her **Boiled Fruit Cake** (page 41). What amazed me is that she made everything by eye, never weighing her ingredients, only using one of those old-fashioned enamel measuring cones if she needed to. I remember everything about those moments: the way she mixed things, how she looked when she was in the kitchen, her pride and love for our family and the pretend telling-off she would give my Grandad when she discovered he had eaten three slices of cake and a choc ice for lunch!

For me, baking comes naturally. I like to think that I got that from Nan. I have always said that if I can be half as good a baker as she was, and half the lady she was, I would be happy.

All of my recipes have a memory to accompany them – this book is my way of letting you into my funny little life! The recipes are inspired by my childhood, my Nan, my Mam and Dad, plus inspiration from the bakeries and cafés we've been to on holidays, and also from developing recipes for my friends' requests, cravings or celebrations.

I love to bake for other people, using their favourite flavours or trying to recall a particular food memory for them. For my Dad this means anything with fresh cream in or on it or added to it. So he loves my **Black Forest Gateau** (page 46) with lashings of extra cream. Mam and my sister love coconut, so fight over my **Coconut, Banana and Dark Chocolate Loaf** (page 57). My brother, on the other hand, always requests a Victoria sponge with fresh strawberries (see the recipe on page 31), while my other half, Liam… well, he'll adore anything Scottish really. So you can thank him for **Tottie Scones** (page 211) and **Macaroni Pies** (page 199)! My Mam's mum, Ivy, had the sweetest tooth (I think her diet was about 95 per cent sugar) so I know I have her to thank for my love of all things sweet. **Ivy's Malteser Ice Cream** (page 148) is here in her honour because I know she would've loved it, and definitely not shared! My pug, Dennis, was key in tasting all the savoury recipes in the book, particularly the **Beef and Ale Pies** (page 186) and **Family Roast Chicken with all the Trimmings** (page 172)!

For me, The Great British Bake Off was the most unforgettable, crazy, incredible experience. It has opened so many doors for me and enabled me to pursue my love of baking, and I cannot thank the programme-makers enough. I went into Bake Off as someone who baked as a hobby but worried a lot about my ability. The programme not only gave me the opportunity to develop my understanding of baking but also enabled me to learn so much. I learnt from my own mistakes but also from the other bakers – who I still call on for advice – and of course from Mary and Paul. Things do still go wrong for me, and sometimes not turn out how I expect, but I don't worry about it now. I just don't tell anyone and I start again! Confidence in baking is so important. I hope that, like me, as you go through this book your confidence will build and you will feel able to change and add things to make these dishes your own.

My favourite things

I unashamedly love a pudding, and always have done (I used to have two puddings for my school lunch – when I was a teacher, too!), and baking recipes that can double up as a pudding are particular favourites. My **Chocolate Hazelnut Brownies** (page 73) and **Mint Chocolate Cake** (page 34) are both perfect examples of this. They can be eaten cold or warmed in the microwave and served in a bowl with a huge scoop of ice cream.

Markets are another of my obsessions. I think this comes from being born and brought up on Edmonton Green (when we lived there, it was a busy, bustling market). I love being able to see, smell and touch fresh fruit and vegetables and to ask questions about meat and fish. What is in season? What is good now? What flavours go with what? Where does this come from? And so on… I encourage you to do this too. Ask questions, touch things, smell things, use local and seasonal produce where you can, and support local and small businesses where possible. Depending on where you live, you could also pick your own wild brambles, plums, nuts and berries. Do check with an expert though, if you are not sure what's what. I'm lucky in that my other half works outdoors and knows a thing or two about foraging!

Another of my passions is vintage and old-fashioned kitchenware and things for the home – French, if possible (I've just bought a set of French brass measuring cups and I have a huge old trunk that's filled with baking bits and pieces). I think vintage items have so much character and look fabulous alongside something you have lovingly baked. I spend a lot of time scouring antique shops and markets looking for my next treasured find. This vintage theme seems to work well with my style of baking – retro and homely bakes with a twist.

All of my favourite recipe books at home are covered in smears and spatters of cake batter, chocolate and icing, and one has even been soaked through to the centre with melted butter! I have folded pages over, written in margins and drawn little diagrams to remind me of how I made the recipes my own. This is what I encourage you to do with this book. I want you to fold the pages over on your favourite recipes and make notes on the pages when you try swapping one ingredient for another or adding your favourite flavour. And draw pictures of the method you use. I want you to make the recipes your own and share them with friends and family. Baking shouldn't be scary, and I hope this book shows you that comforting, delicious and decadent bakes can be made by anyone.

This book is simply me. It is full of the things I like to make and bake, and eat and share with friends and family. I love baking and everything that goes with it: researching ideas, sourcing ingredients, tasting ingredients, preparing and mixing, the evolution from raw to baked, the anticipation of the rise, the heat of the oven and – finally – the finished article, whether it is decorated to within an inch of its life or just sliced and put on a plate before it has had time to even cool! That's the reward you can sit down to enjoy.

Candice
x

Cook's notes

* You might notice that I use teaspoonfuls of chopped garlic and chilli in a lot of my recipes. This is the ready prepared chopped garlic/chilli you can buy in a jar. I use it because I really dislike chopping garlic and chilli. You can of course chop them fresh if you prefer.

* All eggs are free-range medium-sized, unless I state to go large.

* I always use greaseproof paper when lining my tins or baking trays or sheets.

* I always use unsalted butter in my recipes as it means I can control the amount of salt going into the recipe. However, salted butter is a must when spreading on bread.

* I use a free-standing electric mixer or my trusty electric hand whisk when preparing cake mixtures, batters and fillings and to start bread dough off. But all of my recipes can also be made by hand with a whole load of elbow grease.

* All recipes were baked in a fan oven. If you are using a conventional oven, follow the temperatures given after the fan oven temperature in each recipe.

* To melt chocolate for piping, do this in a piping bag (without the metal nozzle) in the microwave, in 20-second bursts. This means less washing up and you can use it straight away.

* If you're freestyling, write everything down as you go. That way if something isn't quite right you can see what you did and change it next time. Guess-the-cake is my favourite thing to do!

Remember: under-whipped cream is better than over-whipped and split!

* You can always salvage a bake. If you have a sunken sponge, cut out smaller pieces and make individual layer cakes. If you have a crack in your roulade, cover it in whipped cream. If your bread has under- or over-proved, don't chuck it: use in a bread and butter pudding (maybe not onion bread though!).

* Take care not to over-whip double cream. I find it stiffens further when it's put into piping bags or spooned out.

* Buy frozen fruit so you can use raspberries and cherries in your bakes all year round. I use them for jams and curds if I can't get fresh and they work brilliantly.

* Break in a new pair of heels when you're baking and moving around the kitchen – it's the perfect time to do so.

* Always have a lipstick to hand. As the incredible Audrey Hepburn once said: 'On a bad day there's always lipstick.'

Store-cupboard essentials

These are the ingredients you'll always want to have to hand!

* golden caster sugar

* light/dark soft brown sugar

* plain and self-raising flour

* strong white bread flour

* baking powder

* bicarbonate of soda

* salt

* smoked paprika

* jarred chopped garlic

* jarred chopped red chilli

* vanilla bean paste

* instant yeast (also called easy-blend and fast-action)

* coconut oil

* wholegrain mustard

Essential kit

* electric scales so measurements are precise

* a good rolling pin – I have my Nan's and it is one of my prized possessions

* a set of teaspoon/tablespoon measures

* a good large mixing bowl

* a wooden spoon

* a whisk

* a spatula

* a palette knife

* disposable piping bags and nozzles

* an electric mixer

I use a free-standing mixer, but handhold is fine too for most things

A bake for every occasion

Whether you are baking with the kids on school holidays and need a few ideas, throwing a party and need some tasty nibbles and bites, or need that a real wow-factor celebration cake that has people fighting for as second slice… I have come up with a few ideas that cover most bake-related situations!

Great to bake with kids

Hidden cherry and lemon cupcakes 58

Apple and pear crumble muffins 61

Peanut butter and marshmallow blondies 66

Nan's butterscotch brownies 68

Chocolate hazelnut brownies 73

Apricot, apple and cashew flapjacks 74

Chewy chocolate orange cookies (opposite) 77

Macadamia nut and raspberry jam biscuits 78

Cornflake tart 97

Chocolate and banana waffles 146

Leave out the alcohol if baking with kids!

Bakes just for grown-ups

Date and ginger cake 37

Lemon, gin and poppy seed cake 40

Piña colada macaroons 87

Cherry Amaretto Bakewell tart 93

Red grapefruit and elderflower sorbet 149

Cointreau and orange hot cross buns 226

Rhubarb syllabub doughnuts 236

Party and celebration bakes

Mocha chocolate cake 30

Triple-layer berry Victoria sponge 31

Carrot cake 38

Black Forest gateau 46

Port-soaked Christmas cake 52

Rhubarb and custard ring 54

Marzipan mince pies 109

Mango and raspberry Pavlova 127

Individual banoffee pies 135

The 3 P's roulade 141

Stilton twisted straws 158

Pork scratchings 162

Perfect for afternoon tea

Raspberry and custard almond cake 50

Nan's boiled fruit cake 41

Lemon and blackberry drizzle loaf 44

Nan's florentines 69

Berry crème tarts 98

Back-to-front chocolate and pear profiteroles 100

Gooseberry fool éclairs 116

Red, white and blue meringues 130

Black pudding sausage rolls 167

Ham hock and chorizo Scotch eggs 171

Vegetable quiche 190

Salmon, prawn and asparagus tart 204

Breakfast, brunch and weekend bakes

Granola 84

Croissants 94

Almond and pear pinwheel pastries 104

Cheese and mushroom Danish rounds 108

Croque monsieur pancakes 208

Tottie scones 211

Apple, walnut and cinnamon buns 230

Ginger and chocolate plait 233

Spiced sultana bagels 240

*All tied up
in some brown paper
with brown string!*

Bakes for gifts

Nan's florentines 69

Orange and hibiscus madeleines (below) 62

Cranberry, orange and hazelnut biscotti 75

Millionaire shortbread hearts 83

Jar of jam 152

Jar of sticky red onion chutney 154

Jar of passion fruit curd 155

I'm not sure if there is anything better than a huge slice of cake.
I think I could eat cake every day for the rest of my life.
I particularly love big, hearty and homely cakes that are made
for sharing. You will find all sorts of cakes in this chapter, from
my **Nan's Boiled Fruit Cake** (page 41), to a grown-up **Lemon,
Gin and Poppy Seed Cake** (page 40) and a big, impressive **Black
Forest Gateau** (page 46). I always taste a raw cake mix before
baking as I think that if it tastes okay raw it will be lovely baked!

When making cakes always ensure that the butter is nice
and soft so it can be incorporated easily into the mixture, and that
the eggs are at room temperature. Never over-beat the mixture
or you will end up with a tough cake. Don't be afraid to play
around with flavours – the basis of a cake will never really change
but the addition of flavour is where you can let your imagination
run wild! Just remember: don't add too much liquid, and roll your
fruit in flour to stop it sinking.

Cakes

Mocha chocolate cake

Courgette in a cake?, I hear you say. Yes, it works and it works well – adding moisture and depth without compromising any of the rich chocolate/coffee flavours. This is a grown-up chocolate cake because the coffee, though not overpowering, gives it an intense flavour. I use ganache in a lot of my recipes. Here, though, by whipping it up after chilling it turns from smooth and dark to fluffy and pale, perfect to complement the dark sponge.

Serves 10–12
—

200g walnut halves
175ml melted coconut oil
300g dark brown
    muscovado sugar
3 eggs
85g cocoa powder
250g plain flour
2 tsp baking powder
1 tsp bicarbonate of soda
1 tsp ground cinnamon
pinch of salt
5 tbsp brewed strong
    black coffee
350g courgettes, grated

Ganache:
500ml double cream
2 tbsp instant coffee
    powder
400g dark chocolate
    (minimum 70% cocoa
    solids), chopped

*Don't just use any old instant coffee. Go for a good-quality coffee as it will make such a difference to the flavour.

Preheat the oven to 150°C fan (170°C/325°F/Gas Mark 3). Grease two 23cm round, loose-bottomed cake tins and line with greaseproof paper.

Spread out the chopped walnuts on a small baking tray and toast in the oven for about 10 minutes. Allow to cool, then roughly chop.

Put the melted oil, sugar and eggs in a large mixing bowl and beat with an electric mixer until combined. Sift the cocoa powder, flour, baking powder, bicarbonate of soda, ground cinnamon and salt into the bowl and mix in.

Pour over the brewed coffee and add the grated courgettes. Mix together until you have a smoothish but courgette-flecked mixture. Fold through half the walnuts.

Divide the mixture between the two prepared tins. Bake for 35–45 minutes until a skewer poked in the middle of each sponge comes out clean. Turn out on to a wire rack. Carefully peel off the lining paper, then leave the sponges to cool completely.

For the ganache, put the cream and coffee powder into a small saucepan set over a low heat and slowly bring to the boil. Meanwhile, put the chocolate in a large bowl. When the cream has started to boil, slowly pour it over the chocolate. Leave for 10 minutes, without touching it, then mix together. This will give you a lovely smooth ganache. Allow the ganache to cool fully, then chill for a couple of hours.

Transfer the cooled and thickened ganache to a free-standing electric mixer fitted with a whisk attachment (or use a handheld electric mixer). Whisk on a medium speed until the ganache goes from a deep brown to a light, whipped pale brown. This will take a couple of minutes.

Spread two-thirds of the whipped ganache on to one of the sponges. Set the second sponge on top. Spread the remaining whipped ganache over the sides and top of the cake – you want an even covering but should still see some of the sponge underneath (a semi-naked look).

Sprinkle the rest of the walnuts in a crescent-moon shape on one side of the top of the cake.

Serve with double cream, whipped if you are feeling fancy.

Triple-layer berry Victoria sponge

A Victoria sponge is always a favourite. You can't really go wrong with a light sponge, fresh fruit and fresh cream. The addition of a middle layer packed with fresh raspberries makes the cake look interesting when you cut into it and also adds a great flavour and texture. This cake is perfect for parties or sharing (I've not known anyone to eat a whole one… yet!).

Serves 10—12

—

335g self-raising flour
335g unsalted butter, softened
335g golden caster sugar
3 tsp baking powder
6 large eggs
grated zest of 2 lemons
juice of 1 lemon
150g fresh raspberries
600ml double cream
500g fresh strawberries, hulled
icing sugar, to finish

Preheat the oven to 160°C fan (180°C/350°F/Gas Mark 4). Grease three 25cm round, loose-bottomed sandwich tins and line the bases with greaseproof paper.

Sift the flour into a large bowl and add the butter, sugar, baking powder, eggs, lemon zest and juice. Mix together until smooth, fluffy and combined. If using an electric mixer, mix on a medium speed and do not over mix.

Divide two-thirds of the mixture between two of the tins. Reserve five of the fresh raspberries for the decoration, then add the rest to the last third of the mixture and mix them through, crushing some of the raspberries as you go. Put this mixture into the third tin.

Place the three tins in the oven and bake for about 20 minutes until the sponges are risen and golden, and are slightly coming away from the edges (try not to open the oven before the 20 minutes are up). The raspberry sponge may need another 5 minutes. Remove the tins from the oven and turn out the sponges on to a wire rack. Leave to cool.

Whip the double cream thick enough to hold its shape – do not over whip. Spoon the cream into a piping bag fitted with a round nozzle.

Continued overleaf

Continued...

Reserve five of the strawberries for the decoration. Evenly slice the rest of the strawberries.

Pipe a layer of double cream on to one of the plain sponges. Top with a layer of sliced strawberries. Spread a small amount of cream on the underside of the raspberry sponge, then place it gently on top of the strawberries (the cream helps the sponges stick together).

Pipe a layer of double cream on the raspberry sponge and top this with the rest of the sliced strawberries. Spread a small amount of cream on the underside of the other plain sponge, then set this on top of the strawberries. Push down gently and check the layers are even.

Top with any leftover cream, the reserved strawberries, cut in half, and the reserved raspberries, then dust with icing sugar.

As this is sandwiched with fresh cream it is a good idea to eat it on the day it is made. It is a huge cake, so is best shared at a party as a fab centrepiece!

*Don't be afraid to vary the flavours for this. Try lime and raspberry, or in the autumn go for blackberry and apple. The basis of the sponge will never change but go nuts with the flavours and decoration.

Mint chocolate cake

Ever eaten those thin, square, minty after-dinner chocolates? Well, I've been told this is like the cake version of them! It is a moist, rich and satisfying cake that can also be served as a warm pudding with ice cream or cream. You can use different oils too – coconut oil is a favourite of mine and rapeseed oil also works.

Serves 10—12
—

130ml light olive oil, plus extra for greasing
200g dark soft brown sugar
3 large eggs
30g cocoa powder (with a high percentage of cocoa solids)
100g mint dark chocolate, chopped into small pieces
140ml boiling water
10 fresh mint leaves, chopped
125g ground almonds
* 25g plain flour
1/2 tsp bicarbonate of soda
pinch of salt
100g white chocolate, to decorate

Preheat the oven to 160°C fan (180°C/350°F/Gas Mark 4). Lightly grease a 25cm springform cake tin and line with greaseproof paper.

Put the oil, sugar and eggs in the bowl of a free-standing electric mixer fitted with a whisk attachment. Beat on a medium speed for about 3 minutes until pale and fluffy.

Combine the cocoa powder, mint chocolate and boiling water in a bowl or jug and stir until the chocolate melts. Mix in the mint.

Whisking the egg and sugar mix on a low speed, slowly pour in the chocolate mixture in a steady stream. Keep whisking until combined. Add the ground almonds, flour, bicarbonate of soda and salt and mix in with a spatula. The mix will be very runny but this is fine.

Pour the mixture into the tin. Bake for 25–30 minutes until a skewer inserted into the middle comes out with just a few sticky crumbs adhering. Remove from the oven and leave to cool in the tin.

Melt the white chocolate in a heatproof bowl set over a saucepan of simmering water. Drizzle the chocolate over the cake to decorate.

*To make this a gluten-free cake, simply omit the flour and increase the ground almonds to 150g.

Date & ginger cake

My own Jamaican ginger cake – sticky, rich, spicy and moist! The dates give it an almost toffee-like texture and the lemon is a zesty little surprise. Be sure not to overcook this as you'll lose all the sticky loveliness.

Serves 10

—

150g unsalted butter
125g dark muscovado sugar
200g golden syrup
200g dark treacle
4 tsp grated fresh ginger
2 tsp ground ginger
1 tsp ground cinnamon
75g stoneless dates, finely chopped
finely grated zest of 1 lemon (keep the lemon for the decoration)
1 tsp bicarbonate of soda
100ml fiery ginger beer
150–200ml whole milk
2 large eggs
300g plain flour
pinch of salt

To decorate:

5 dates
3 pieces stem ginger

Preheat the oven to 150°C fan (170°C/325°F/Gas Mark 3). Grease a 25cm springform cake tin and line with greaseproof paper.

Melt the butter with the sugar, golden syrup, treacle, grated fresh and ground ginger, cinnamon, chopped dates and lemon zest in a saucepan over a low/medium heat, stirring occasionally. Remove from the heat.

Mix the bicarbonate of soda with 2 tablespoons of the ginger beer, then add to the pan along with the rest of the ginger beer, the milk and eggs. Sift the flour and salt into the pan and whisk until all lumps have dissolved and you have a smooth, runny batter.

Pour into the tin. Bake for 45–60 minutes until the cake has risen and feels firm to a light touch on top but a bit sticky (slightly undercooked is better as the cake will be stickier). Leave to cool before removing from the tin. Turn the oven down to 100°C fan (120°C/250°F/Gas Mark ½).

Slice the lemon (kept after zesting) into 3mm slices. Arrange in one layer on a baking sheet and place in the oven. Leave to dry out for 1–2 hours.

Slice the dates and stem ginger lengthways.

Arrange the lemon slices on top of the cake and scatter the date and ginger slices over the surface.

Carrot cake

My most favourite, number-one choice in cake. I will always choose a carrot cake if I go to a bakery or café, and I barely let this one cool enough to frost before I'm diving in for a huge slice! The pineapple and banana make this cake so moist and give it an almost tropical flavour alongside the coconut. There are so many textures and flavours in this cake – it is big, bold and bloody delicious!

Serves 10–12

—

300g unsalted butter, softened
150g dark soft brown sugar
200g light soft brown sugar
3 large eggs
1 tsp vanilla bean paste
225g plain flour
1/2 tsp bicarbonate of soda
1/2 tsp baking powder
2 tsp ground cinnamon
1/2 tsp freshly grated nutmeg
200g peeled and grated carrots (about 2 carrots)
75g drained canned pineapple in juice, chopped and crushed
1 small ripe banana, mashed
100g desiccated coconut
grated zests of 1 orange and 1 lemon
50g pecan nuts, chopped
100g sultanas

Preheat the oven to 140°C fan (160°C/325°F/Gas Mark 3). Grease a 25cm springform cake tin and line with greaseproof paper.

In a large bowl beat together the butter, both types of sugar, the eggs and vanilla with an electric mixer until smooth (if the mixture starts to curdle add a little of the flour). Sift the flour, bicarbonate of soda, baking powder, cinnamon and nutmeg into the bowl and mix until combined.

Mix in the grated carrots, crushed pineapple, mashed banana, coconut and orange and lemon zests. Finally, fold in the chopped pecans and the sultanas.

Pour the cake mixture into the prepared tin and level the top with a spatula. Bake for 1 – 1 1/2 hours until a skewer inserted into the middle comes out clean (if the top starts to brown too much, cover with foil). Remove from the oven and allow to cool in the tin.

Make the brittle while the cake is baking. Put the whole pecans in a frying pan and toast lightly until golden brown. Chop roughly, then spread out on a baking tray. Heat the sugar and 4 tablespoons of water in a small pan over a medium heat until the sugar has dissolved. When the syrup starts to bubble, allow it to turn a golden amber colour (do not stir), then pour it over the chopped nuts. Sprinkle on the rock salt. Leave to cool and set.

Pecan brittle:
100g pecan nuts
100g golden caster sugar
rock salt

Frosting:
50g unsalted butter,
   softened
300g icing sugar, sifted
½ tsp ground cinnamon
100g full-fat soft cheese

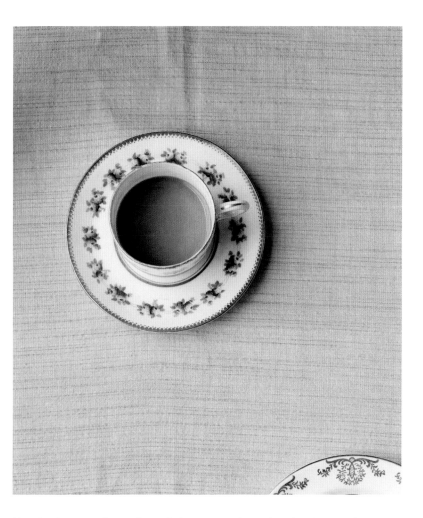

For the frosting, beat the soft butter in a large bowl using an electric mixer until smooth. Gradually add the icing sugar, beating between additions. Add the cinnamon. Beat in the soft cheese a little at a time until the mix is smooth and light and not too runny – you may not need all of the soft cheese. Take care not to over mix.

Spread the soft cheese frosting over the whole cake – top and sides – using a palette knife. Shatter the pecan brittle by either hitting it with a sharp knife, or dropping it on to a hard work surface, to get shards. Scatter the pecan brittle shards over the frosting.

* You don't need to add frosting to the cake, or the pecan brittle, but wowee they make it pretty!

Lemon, gin & poppy seed cake

For the gin lover in your life, here's a naughty alternative to a lemon drizzle cake. Using a really good-quality gin does make a difference – coming from someone who didn't drink gin until last year, trust me on this. The gin doesn't give an overpowering flavour but just leaves a warm aftertaste that gives you a big hug as you devour your slice of cake!

Serves 8–10
—
225g self-raising flour
225g unsalted butter, softened
225g golden caster sugar
2 tsp baking powder
4 eggs
grated zest of 1 lemon
grated zest of 1 lime
juice of ½ lemon
40g poppy seeds

Syrup:
60ml gin
juice of 2 lemons
50g caster sugar
20g granulated sugar

Preheat the oven to 160°C fan (180°C/350°F/Gas Mark 4). Grease a 25cm springform cake tin (I use a heart-shaped silicone tin).

Put the flour, butter, sugar, baking powder, eggs, citrus zests, lemon juice and poppy seeds in a large bowl. Using an electric mixer or a hand whisk, beat together until smooth and fluffy.

Pour the mixture into the prepared tin and bake for 45–50 minutes until the sponge is cooked – a skewer inserted into the middle should come out clean. Remove from the oven.

Heat the gin, lemon juice and sugar in a small saucepan over a low/medium heat, stirring until the sugar has dissolved. When the syrup starts to bubble around the edges remove from the heat.

Poke holes all over the top of the sponge using a skewer (do not go all the way through to the bottom). Slowly pour the hot syrup over the still-warm sponge, allowing it to absorb the syrup.

Sprinkle the granulated sugar evenly over the top. Allow to cool completely before removing from the tin.

If making this cake for children, or if you just want to leave out the alcohol, replace the gin with the juice of a lime for a tangy kick.

You can put this cake into any tin shape you like. It works well as a layer cake too – simply divide the mixture between two sandwich tins and bake for 20–25 minutes; when cold, sandwich with lemon curd and buttercream.

Nan's boiled fruit cake

This is my Nan's exact recipe – I converted the quantities to grams as Nan had written it in ounces, cups and litres. It was one of my Grandad's favourites. My Nan always used margarine, but you can swap it for unsalted butter if you prefer.

Serves 8–10

—

340g mixed dried fruit (I use 100g sultanas, 90g raisins, 50g chopped dried apricots, 50g dried cranberries, 25g mixed peel and 25g chopped glacé cherries)

75g walnuts, chopped

225g golden caster sugar (or a mix of light soft brown sugar and caster sugar)

115g margarine

225g self-raising flour

pinch of salt

½ tsp mixed spice

2 large eggs, beaten

Preheat the oven to 140°C fan (160°C/325°F/Gas Mark 3). Grease a 900g (2lb) loaf tin and line with greaseproof paper.

Combine the fruit, walnuts, sugar, margarine and 235ml water in a heavy-based saucepan and heat very gently for 10 minutes, stirring occasionally to dissolve the sugar. Remove from the heat and cool to blood temperature.

Stir in the flour, salt, mixed spice and beaten eggs. Mix well.

Transfer to the tin. Bake for 1½–2 hours until a skewer inserted into the middle comes out clean. Allow to cool in the tin before turning out. Store in an airtight tin.

Photo overleaf →

Lemon & blackberry drizzle loaf

We love walking our dog, Dennis, and where we live we are lucky enough to have lots of fresh brambles growing. So come autumn we take a bag with us on walks and collect brambles. (We don't pick the ones that are close to the ground!) Adding them whole to this loaf means you get a burst of blackberry juice when you take a bite – tart but sweet perfection.

Serves 8–10
—

115g self-raising flour
1 tsp baking powder
115g unsalted butter,
    softened
165g golden caster sugar
2 medium eggs
3 lemons
1 tsp fresh lemon thyme
    leaves
150g blackberries

To finish:
about 50g icing sugar
10 blackberries
shreds of lemon zest
fresh lemon thyme sprigs

Preheat the oven to 160°C fan (180°C/350°F/Gas Mark 4). Grease a 450g (1 lb) loaf tin and line with greaseproof paper.

Sift the flour and baking powder into a large bowl and add the soft butter and 115g of the caster sugar, along with the eggs. Grate the zest from two of the lemons into the bowl. Squeeze the juice from half of the third lemon and add along with the lemon thyme leaves. Beat with an electric mixer just until smooth and light (take care not to over mix).

Fold in the blackberries.

Pour the mixture into the tin. Bake for 45–50 minutes until a skewer inserted into the middle of the cake comes out clean (avoid skewering a blackberry). Remove from the oven and set aside to cool slightly while you make the syrup.

Squeeze the juice from the two lemons you zested and pour into a small saucepan. Add the remaining 50g caster sugar. Set over a medium heat and stir until the sugar has dissolved to make a syrup. Turn the heat up slightly and let the syrup bubble away for a couple of minutes.

Using a skewer, poke holes all over the top of the still-warm cake, then slowly pour the lemon syrup all over the surface so it penetrates right through the sponge. Leave to cool fully.

Squeeze the juice from the remaining lemon half into a small bowl and stir in enough icing sugar to make a smooth, runny icing.

Once the loaf is cold, drizzle over the icing and top with fresh blackberries, shreds of lemon zest and tiny picked sprigs of lemon thyme.

You can toss the blackberries in a little flour before you fold them in, if you want to prevent them from sinking in the cake; I don't mind this as I think it adds to the charm.

Black Forest gateau

Retro at its best: rich, dark and moist chocolate sponges with Kirsch-soaked cherries and – my Dad's favourite ingredient – lots and lots of cream. This is a beast of a cake so make it when you want to impress a lot of people. My decorations are just a guideline – you can decorate however you like. Because of the fresh cream the cake is best eaten on the same day, but chances are that once people have a slice it won't last long anyway.

Serves 10–12

—

400g plain flour
4 tbsp cocoa powder
2 tsp bicarbonate of soda
2 tsp baking powder
225g golden caster sugar
100g dark soft brown sugar
40g ground almonds
335ml melted coconut oil
4 tbsp golden syrup
335ml whole milk
4 large eggs

Filling:
400g frozen black cherries, thawed
150ml Kirsch
2 tbsp golden caster sugar
400ml double cream
1 tsp vanilla bean paste

Ganache:
200ml double cream
200g dark chocolate (minimum 70% cocoa solids), chopped

Preheat the oven to 160°C fan (180°C/350°F/Gas Mark 4). Grease three 20cm round sandwich tins and line with greaseproof paper.

Sift the flour, cocoa powder, bicarbonate of soda and baking powder into a mixing bowl. Stir in both types of sugar and the ground almonds. Make a well in the middle. Pour the melted coconut oil, golden syrup, milk and eggs into the well. Using an electric mixer, beat on low/medium speed until everything is well combined and smooth.

Divide the mixture equally between the three tins. Bake for 25–30 minutes until the sponges are springy to a light touch in the centre. Cool in the tins for a few minutes, then turn out on to a wire rack. Peel off the lining paper before leaving to cool fully.

To make the filling, put the cherries, Kirsch and sugar into a small saucepan and heat over a low/medium heat for about 5 minutes, until the sugar has completely dissolved and the mixture is bubbling. Remove from the heat and allow to cool.

Whip the double cream with the vanilla in a large bowl until just thick. Spoon into a piping bag fitted with a large round nozzle. Keep in the fridge until needed.

For the ganache, pour the cream into a saucepan and heat over a medium heat until small bubbles appear round the edge. Take the pan off the heat and add the chocolate. Leave for 10 minutes before mixing until smooth. Chill to thicken up slightly.

Place the milk and white chocolate in two separate small heatproof bowls and melt in the microwave in 30-second bursts. Lay a piece of greaseproof paper on a baking sheet. Using either a teaspoon, or a small piping bag with a fine nozzle or opening, drizzle/pipe the milk chocolate into various sizes of tree shapes, stars and swirls. They don't have to be perfect, just shaped. Repeat with the white chocolate. Place the shapes in the fridge to set.

50g milk chocolate
50g white chocolate
100g fresh cherries (with
    stalks if possible)
50g dark chocolate
    (minimum 70% cocoa
    solids)
icing sugar, for dusting
    (optional)

Place one of the cooled sponges on a board or serving plate. Make a few holes in the sponge using a skewer, then spread a third of the black cherry and Kirsch filling over the surface so the liquid seeps into the sponge. Pipe a layer of vanilla cream over the cherries.

Turn a second sponge over and spread a layer of ganache on its base, then place this – ganache-side down – on top of the cherries and cream.

Poke holes in the top of the second sponge, then spread half of the remaining cherry and Kirsch filling over the surface. Pipe a layer of vanilla cream over the cherries.

Spread a layer of ganache on the base of the third sponge, then place on top, ganache-side down. Poke holes in this sponge, then drizzle over just the juice from the remaining filling (reserve the cherries). Pipe or spoon little mounds of vanilla cream on the top sponge, in concentric rings, gradually making the cream mounds taller as you get to the centre.

Put the remaining ganache into a piping bag fitted with a star nozzle and pipe small star shapes in between the cream rings and around the central cream mound.

Place the reserved Kirsch-soaked cherries on top of the cream, adding a pile of fresh cherries in the centre.

Set a white chocolate shape on each ganache star, grate the dark chocolate all over the top and finish with a dusting of icing sugar (if using).

Photo overleaf →

Raspberry & custard almond cake

This is a moist, squishy cake that can be served warm with extra custard
or cold as a delicious slice. It is a fairly light sponge but the addition
of creamy custard, almonds and sharp-sweet raspberries means it all
sinks in together to make a layer of delightful stodge. Yes please!

Serves 8 hungry people
—

400g fresh raspberries
250ml Vanilla Custard
    (page 121)
250g unsalted butter,
    softened
150g golden caster sugar
100g light soft brown
    sugar
4 large eggs
200g plain flour
50g ground almonds
125ml whole milk
2 tsp baking powder
grated zest of 1 orange
30g flaked almonds
icing sugar, to finish
    (optional)

Preheat the oven to 160°C fan (180°C/350°F/Gas Mark 4). Grease a
23cm springform cake tin and line with greaseproof paper.

Set aside 100g raspberries for decoration. Put 200g of the remaining
raspberries in a small bowl and crush them. Fold the crushed
raspberries through the custard.

Combine the butter, both types of sugar, eggs, flour, ground almonds,
milk, baking powder and orange zest in a large bowl and beat together
with an electric mixer until combined and smooth. Fold in the remaining
100g raspberries – it is a good thing if some of them are crushed.

Tip half the sponge mixture into the greased and lined cake tin and top
with the raspberry-swirled custard. Pour the other half of the sponge
mixture over the top of the custard and spread out evenly. Scatter the
flaked almonds over the surface.

Bake for 1–1¼ hours. Test after 1 hour by inserting a skewer into the
middle – if it comes out clean, the cake is done. Remove from the oven
and allow to cool in the tin for about 1½ hours before turning out on
to a wire rack to cool fully.

Serve with the reserved raspberries and decorate the cake with a
dusting of icing sugar, if you like.

Port-soaked Christmas cake

Every year my Nan would make a Christmas cake with the icing pulled up in small peaks so it looked like snow. She always decorated the top with the same little decorations – a snowman, Santa on his sledge, a reindeer – and tied a red ribbon around the base. When she passed away I took over making the cake, a task I found very daunting. Mine will never be as good as hers but I give it a good go and I know she would be proud of me. With all that port, my Grandad would have loved a big slice. This is a lengthy recipe but, come Christmas and probably for a good few weeks after, it will be so worth it! And, as with most things, it really does get better with age: start making it at least a month before Christmas, ideally two.

Serves a lot of people!
—

200g raisins
200g sultanas
100g dried apricots,
    roughly chopped
100g dried cherries, halved
100g dried cranberries
100g stoneless dates,
    chopped
75g brazil nuts, roughly
    chopped
1 cinnamon stick
100g mixed candied peel
grated zest and juice of
    1 orange
150ml port, plus extra
    for soaking
150g unsalted butter,
    softened
150g dark soft brown sugar
4 large eggs, beaten
175g plain flour
1 tsp baking powder
1 tsp ground cinnamon
1 tsp ground ginger
1 tsp mixed spice
1 tsp freshly grated
    nutmeg
pinch of salt
50g ground almonds

The night before you are going to bake the cake, put the raisins, sultanas, apricots, cherries, cranberries, dates, brazil nuts, cinnamon stick and mixed peel into a large bowl. Add the orange zest and juice, then add the port. Give everything a good mix together, then cover with cling film and leave to soak overnight.

Next day, preheat the oven to 130°C fan (150°C/300°F/Gas Mark 2). Grease a 25cm springform cake tin (make sure it has high sides), then double line both the bottom and sides with greaseproof paper.

In a large mixing bowl beat together the butter and sugar with an electric mixer until pale and fluffy. Add the eggs a little at a time, beating well after each addition. If the mixture starts to curdle add a spoonful of the flour.

Sift in the flour, baking powder, cinnamon, ginger, mixed spice and nutmeg. Add the salt and fold through the ground almonds.

Remove the cinnamon stick from the port-soaked fruit, then tip it all into the mixing bowl. Fold into the cake mixture. Make sure everything is evenly mixed.

Pour into the prepared cake tin and smooth the surface. Make the sides slightly higher than the centre to prevent a mound appearing during baking. Place in the oven and bake for 1 hour.

Cover the cake with foil, then bake for a further 1–2 hours. Check with a skewer inserted into the middle after 2 hours of total baking time – the cake is done if the skewer comes out clean. If the skewer comes out with batter stuck to it, return it to the oven and bake for a further 15 minutes then check again (you may need to repeat this – the cake can need up to 3 hours in the oven).

Remove from the oven and allow to cool fully in the tin.

Marzipan:
200g golden caster sugar
220g icing sugar, plus
 extra for dusting
200g ground almonds
1 tsp almond extract
2 eggs
apricot preserve,
 for sticking

Royal icing:
2 large egg whites
500g icing sugar
1 tsp glycerine
1 tsp lemon juice

Poke a few holes in the top of the cooled cake and carefully dribble over some extra port. Allow to soak in before wrapping tightly with greaseproof paper and foil, tied on with string. Leave in an airtight tin for a week.

Feed the cake with more port as before, then wrap and leave for another week. Repeat the process every week until Christmas (a minimum of four weeks, ideally eight weeks).

When the cake is ready to be iced, make the marzipan. Mix both types of sugar with the ground almonds in a large bowl, then rub in the almond extract. Make a well in the middle and crack in the eggs. Cut the eggs into the dry ingredients using a blunt knife.

Turn out on to a work surface dusted with icing sugar. Knead briefly with your hands to make a smooth paste (don't let it get too warm or it will be greasy). Add a bit more icing sugar if the marzipan seems too wet. Roll out the marzipan on the sugared surface to 4mm thick.

Gently heat the apricot preserve until melted, then pass through a sieve. Brush this apricot glaze all over the cake.

Gently lift up the marzipan with the help of the rolling pin and drape it over the cake. Smooth the marzipan down with your hands, ensuring there are no air bubbles. Trim off any excess marzipan from around the bottom edge of the cake.

To make the royal icing, put the egg whites in a large bowl and whisk with an electric mixer until they hold soft peaks. Gradually sift in the icing sugar, whisking, until smooth and stiff peaks form. Add the glycerine and lemon juice and whisk through.

Using a palette knife, spread the icing over the marzipan however you prefer – I like to ice it in peaky swirls, like a snow scene.

The cake is now ready to decorate with Christmas bows, ribbons and any little ornaments you have (decorate the cake before the icing has set).

* You can use whatever alcohol you like to feed the cake — whisky, brandy or for a different flavour a dark rum. I just prefer the rich berry of port.

Rhubarb & custard ring

Rhubarb and custard, a retro sweet shop classic and one of my and my Mam's favourite flavour combos. Forced rhubarb has a beautiful pink colour but I always think rhubarb is at its very best when it's in season. You can also serve this as a warm pudding – scatter a few more flaked almonds on it and drench in more custard. If you don't have a ring cake tin you can make this in a normal springform tin. Just be time wary.

Serves 10
—

185g unsalted butter, softened, plus extra for the tin
150g fresh rhubarb
juice of ½ orange
185g self-raising flour
40g ground almonds
185g golden caster sugar
3 large eggs
1½ tsp baking powder
finely grated zest of 1 orange, plus extra shreds of zest to serve
20g demerara sugar
150g Vanilla Custard (page 121)
icing sugar, for dusting

Poached rhubarb:
100g fresh rhubarb, cut into 1cm-thick slices
1 tsp golden caster sugar

Preheat the oven to 160°C fan (180°C/350°F/Gas Mark 4). Using soft butter, grease well a 25cm fluted ring cake tin (bundt tin).

Chop the rhubarb into small pieces and place three-quarters in a small saucepan with the orange juice. Cook over a low heat until softened slightly. Allow to cool.

In a large bowl combine the flour, almonds, butter, golden caster sugar, eggs, baking powder and orange zest and beat with an electric mixer until well combined and fluffy.

Using a slotted spoon, add the softened rhubarb to the mix – leave the juice in the pan (keep this) – and fold through.

Scatter the remaining uncooked rhubarb over the bottom of the tin and sprinkle the demerara sugar on top. Pour two-thirds of the sponge mixture over the rhubarb, then spoon the custard on top. Cover with the remaining sponge mix.

Bake for 45 minutes, then test by inserting a skewer into the cake – it will be very moist due to the custard but when cooked the skewer will come out clean, save for a few crumbs and custard. If necessary, continue baking for a further 10–15 minutes.

Remove from the oven and allow to cool completely in the tin.

To make the poached rhubarb, place the sliced rhubarb in a saucepan with the sugar and 1 tablespoon of water and poach over a low heat for 3–4 minutes until the rhubarb has started to soften but still keeps its shape. Remove from the heat.

Once the cake is cool, turn it out upside down onto a plate and drizzle over the reserved rhubarb juice from the pan. Top the cake with the poached rhubarb and strands of orange zest and dust with icing sugar to serve.

Coconut, banana & dark chocolate loaf

I am a nightmare for letting bananas get overripe – I only really like to eat them green. This is a great recipe for using those poor overripe bananas that I haven't got round to eating! There won't be a huge rise on this loaf but that's because it is super moist and packed with banana and coconut. This is a great quick cake if you are short on time. You can cover it in frosting too, if you want to dress it up!

Serves 8
—
2 ripe bananas
70g plain flour
½ tsp bicarbonate of soda
½ tsp baking powder
15g cocoa powder
50g unsalted butter, softened
75g dark soft brown sugar
1 large egg
1 tbsp whole milk
50g desiccated coconut
75g dark chocolate (minimum 70% cocoa solids)
1 banana, cut in half lengthways

To decorate:
25g coconut flakes
100g dark chocolate (minimum 70% cocoa solids)

Preheat the oven to 160°C fan (180°C/350°F/Gas Mark 4). Grease a 450g (1 lb) loaf tin and line with greaseproof paper.

Put the peeled bananas in a large mixing bowl and mash them with a fork or beat using an electric mixer. Sift the flour, bicarbonate of soda, baking powder and cocoa powder into the bowl and add the soft butter, sugar, egg and milk. Mix until well combined using a wooden spoon or the mixer. Fold in the desiccated coconut.

Using a sharp knife, chop the dark chocolate into small irregular pieces. Add to the cake mixture and fold in until evenly distributed. Pour into the lined loaf tin. If using, lay the banana halves, cut-side up, on top. Bake for 40–50 minutes – test by inserting a skewer in the middle of the loaf; the skewer should come out clean. Leave to cool in the tin for a few minutes before turning out on to a wire rack to cool fully.

Place the flaked coconut in a cold frying pan and gently toast over a low heat until slightly golden. (Keep the coconut moving in the pan and watch carefully as the coconut will brown quickly.) Tip on to a piece of kitchen paper and allow to cool.

Melt the dark chocolate in a heatproof bowl set over a pan of boiling water. Drizzle the melted chocolate over the top of the loaf, then sprinkle on the toasted flaked coconut.

Hidden cherry & lemon cupcakes

These quick and easy cupcakes are perfect to make with the kids on a weekend or to take to work for cheeky elevenses. I like the hidden surprise of the cherry in the sponge – an unassuming, pretty cupcake with a little treat inside! The beauty of frozen cherries is that you can get the juiciness of fresh cherries whenever you like.

Makes 12

—

225g self-raising flour
225g golden caster sugar
225g unsalted butter,
    softened
4 eggs
2 tsp baking powder
grated zest and juice of
    1 lemon
about 24 frozen black
    cherries, thawed

Buttercream:
225g unsalted butter,
    softened
500g icing sugar
grated zest and juice of
    1 lemon, plus extra
    grated zest to decorate
about 25g full-fat soft
    cheese
red food colouring gel
6 fresh cherries, halved
    and stones removed

Preheat the oven to 160°C fan (180°C/350°F/Gas Mark 4). Place paper cupcake cases in 12 muffin tin holes.

Put the flour, sugar, butter, eggs, baking powder, lemon zest and juice in a large bowl and mix together with an electric mixer until combined and fluffy.

Spoon the mixture into the cupcake cases, filling each two-thirds full. Push a thawed frozen cherry into the centre of each one. Bake for 20–25 minutes until risen and golden. Remove from the tin to a wire rack and leave to cool.

To make the buttercream, put the soft butter in a large bowl and beat with an electric mixer until pale. Sift in the icing sugar and add the lemon zest, then continue to beat until combined. The mixture will be quite stiff at this point so slowly add the soft cheese a teaspoon at a time and enough of the lemon juice to make a smooth and fluffy buttercream (it should not be gritty). I prefer buttercream to be soft but still able to hold a good shape.

Fit a star nozzle on a piping bag. Add a drop of red food colouring gel to the top of the bag and allow to trickle down inside. Spoon the buttercream into the piping bag.

Pipe buttercream in a rose shape on the top of each cupcake.

Place a fresh cherry half or two on top of each swirl and grate over some fresh lemon zest.

* You could always use a whole fresh cherry on top with the stalk sticking out — just remind people not to swallow the stone! — or try popping a thawed cherry in the buttercream, piping around it and over it on the cakes to make a hidden surprise!

Apple & pear crumble muffins

A common theme in this book is my love of puddings, especially when two puddings are combined in one recipe. These muffins, flavoured with apple and pear, have a secret centre of vanilla custard to contrast with the crunchy texture of a crumble on top. The fruit content might make you think you are being quite good but actually the muffins are rather naughty!

Makes 12
—

1 large Bramley apple
1 large Conference pear
1 tbsp light soft brown sugar
1/2 tsp ground cinnamon
25g unsalted butter

Crumble topping:
25g plain flour
35g light soft brown sugar
25g cold unsalted butter
25g rolled oats

Muffin mixture:
250g unsalted butter, softened
150g golden caster sugar
250g self-raising flour
1/2 tsp baking powder
4 large eggs
1 tsp vanilla extract
1/2 tsp ground cinnamon
about 150ml Vanilla Custard (page 121)

Preheat the oven to 160°C fan (180°C/350°F/Gas Mark 4). Line a 12-hole muffin tin with paper muffin cases.

Peel, core and chop the apples and pears and spread them out on a baking tray. Sprinkle over the sugar and cinnamon, and dab the butter on. Place in the oven and cook for 15–20 minutes, stirring around once about halfway through to coat all the fruit with the buttery juices. The fruit should be just starting to soften. Remove and leave to cool. Leave the oven on.

For the crumble topping, mix the flour and brown sugar in a large bowl. Drop lumps of the butter into the mix and rub together using your fingertips, until the mixture resembles breadcrumbs. Mix in the oats, squeezing the mix together so you have uneven lumps of crumble.

To make the sponge mixture for the muffins, put the soft butter, sugar, flour, baking powder, eggs, vanilla and cinnamon in another large bowl. Mix with an electric mixer on a medium speed, or with a whisk or wooden spoon, until combined and creamy. Fold in the apple and pear mix with a little of the juices.

Spoon a layer of the sponge mix into each muffin case to about half full. Make a little well in the mix. Spoon 2 teaspoons of custard into the well and cover with more sponge mix. Sprinkle with the crumble topping. Place in the oven and bake for 25–30 minutes – check by inserting a skewer into one of the muffins; the skewer should come out clean (the muffins will still be very moist) – there may be some custard on the skewer.

Allow to cool in the tin for a couple of minutes before transferring the muffins to a wire rack to cool fully.

Orange & hibiscus madeleines

I love France, everything and anything French, and j'adore Paris! I first tried madeleines on a school trip to France and loved the simplicity of them along with a bowl of hot chocolate. Now when I make them, they are barely out of the oven before I'm shovelling one into my mouth! Orange adds a lovely citrus taste and the hibiscus almost a berry/rose-like touch. Hibiscus is great in tea too!

Makes about 32

—

1 tbsp dried hibiscus petals
100ml boiling water
90g unsalted butter, melted and cooled, plus extra to grease the moulds
50g soft light brown sugar
100g golden caster sugar
2 large eggs
grated zest and juice of 1 orange, plus extra zest to decorate
100g plain flour, plus extra for the moulds
just under 1 tsp baking powder
pinch of salt
1 tbsp orange blossom honey

Put the dried hibiscus petals in a small bowl and pour over the boiling water. Leave to soften for about 5 minutes.

Meanwhile, brush your madeleine moulds with melted butter, then dust them lightly with flour.

Combine the brown sugar, 50g of the caster sugar and the eggs in a large bowl and whisk with an electric hand whisk until light and fluffy. Add the orange zest, 90g cooled melted butter, plain flour, baking powder, salt, honey and 1 tablespoon of the hibiscus water, and mix together to make a batter. Leave for a minimum of 30 minutes.

Preheat the oven to 170°C fan (190°C/375°F/Gas Mark 5).

Spoon the batter into the prepared madeleine moulds (you will need to bake in batches). Take care not to overfill the moulds. Bake for 10–12 minutes until risen and golden.

Remove the madeleines from the moulds and place on a wire rack. Cool the moulds, then brush with melted butter and dust with flour again before baking another batch of madeleines.

Once all the madeleines have been baked and cooled, mix together the orange juice, the remaining 50g caster sugar and 3 tablespoons of the hibiscus water in a small saucepan. Stir over a medium heat until the sugar has dissolved and you have a thick syrup.

Poke a hole in the underside of each madeleine and brush over the syrup. Wait for this to soak in, then brush on a second coat of the syrup. Finish with a grating of orange zest. These are best eaten fresh on the day of baking.

I like to call the treats in this chapter the BBTs! There is something here for everyone – a luscious variety of brownies and blondies, flapjacks, biscotti and decadently rich, caramel-filled shortbread. Some recipes are quick and easy whilst others take a little more time but are totally worth it and certain to become firm favourites. I normally use a square or rectangular tin for brownies and blondies, which means there can be a fight for the squidgy middle square. To avoid this, you could bake them in a round tin – that way each slice will have some of the soft, gooey middle.

You will find I've used a variety of sugars in this chapter. I love the way different sugars give different textures and flavours. Have a play around yourself – why not mix a few different sugars together? Baking is supposed to be fun and this chapter is the place to experiment.

Brownies, biscuits & traybakes

Peanut butter & marshmallow blondies

The brownie's blonde best mate! This is actually my best friend, Anna – she's the blondie and I'm the brownie. Don't be tempted to overbake these or they will lose that gooey centre. The marshmallows on top are sticky, stretchy and sweet, a perfect match to the crunchy and ever so slightly salty peanut butter.

Makes 12 squares

—

175g unsalted butter, melted

300g light soft brown sugar

200g crunchy peanut butter

2 large eggs

1 tsp vanilla bean paste

200g plain flour

1 tsp baking powder

pinch of salt

150g dark chocolate (minimum 70% cocoa solids), cut into rough chunks

200g pink and white marshmallows

Preheat the oven to 160°C fan (180°C/350°F/Gas Mark 4). Line a 20cm square baking tin with greaseproof paper.

Mix together the melted butter and sugar until the sugar has dissolved. Add the peanut butter and mix until combined. Beat in the eggs and vanilla bean paste.

Sift the flour, baking powder and salt into the bowl and fold to combine. Stir through the chunks of chocolate.

Pour the mixture into the lined tin. Place the marshmallows in rows on top of the mix.

Bake for 50–60 minutes until risen. The marshmallows will have toasted golden and melted so will be very sticky. Remove from the oven and leave to cool fully in the tin.

Once cold, lift out of the tin, using the paper to help, and cut into squares.

Nan's butterscotch brownies

Another perfect little recipe from my Nan, tucked away in her little book. These rich and chewy brownies will satisfy even the sweetest tooth! They work brilliantly as the base for my Coconut Layers (see page 86) if you fancied something a little different.

Makes 12 squares
—

55g unsalted butter
170g light soft brown sugar
2 eggs
85g plain flour
1 tsp baking powder
55g walnuts, chopped
85g chocolate chips

Topping:
55g golden caster sugar
85ml evaporated milk
110g dark chocolate
    (minimum 70% cocoa
    solids), broken into
    pieces
30g unsalted butter,
    cut into cubes
85g walnuts, chopped

Preheat the oven to 160°C fan (180°C/350°F/Gas Mark 4). Line a 25cm square baking tin with greaseproof paper.

Melt the butter and sugar together in a saucepan over a low heat until bubbly. Remove from the heat and allow to cool slightly, then beat in the eggs followed by the flour and baking powder. Stir in the walnuts and chocolate chips.

Pour into the lined tin and bake for 25–30 minutes until the the top is shiny and crisp. The brownie should be gooey in the middle – insert a skewer into the middle and it should come out with some mixture still stuck to it, but if you insert it at the edge of the brownie it should come out clean. Allow to cool in the tin, then turn out on to a wire rack.

For the topping, heat the sugar with the evaporated milk in a saucepan, stirring to dissolve the sugar. Bring to the boil, then turn the heat down and simmer for 6 minutes. Remove from the heat. Add the chocolate and butter and stir until melted and smooth. Pour into a bowl and chill for 2 hours.

Spread the thickened topping over the cooled brownie. Sprinkle the chopped walnuts over the top. Cut into squares.

Nan's florentines

This is another handwritten recipe from my Nan. It was perfect the very first time I made it (that says it all really) and so was she. Feel free to change the fruit and nuts if you want, although why would you when it's perfect the way she wrote it?

Makes 38–40

—

60g unsalted butter
170g golden caster sugar
30g plain flour
150ml double cream
115g flaked almonds
115g whole toasted
    almonds or pecans,
    roughly chopped
85g flaked coconut
85g dried apricots,
    chopped
60g dried cherries
200g dark chocolate
    (minimum 70% cocoa
    solids), broken into
    pieces

Preheat the oven to 170°C fan (190°C/375°F/Gas Mark 5).

Melt the butter with the sugar in a saucepan over a low heat. When the sugar has dissolved and the liquid is golden and bubbling, add the flour and mix until smooth over a low heat. Remove from the heat and slowly add the cream, stirring the whole time until smooth and glossy.

Add the flaked almonds, chopped almonds or pecans, coconut flakes, apricots and cherries and mix well until everything is combined and covered with the creamy mixture.

Line four baking sheets with greaseproof paper. Drop the mixture in heaped teaspoonfuls on to the greaseproof paper, ensuring there is about 2cm between each heap of mixture.

Place in the preheated oven near the top and bake for 12–15 minutes (switch the baking sheets around halfway through).

Remove from the oven and allow to cool for 3–4 minutes before transferring to a wire rack – use a flat palette knife to move the florentines. Leave to cool completely.

Melt the dark chocolate in a heatproof bowl set over a saucepan of simmering water until melted and smooth. Coat the flat underside of each florentine with chocolate and allow to set slightly before zigzagging a fork across the chocolate to make a pattern. Then leave, chocolate-side up, to set completely.

This was my Nan's recipe but she had written it in ounces. I have converted to grams to make it easier for you. It took me a while to decipher!

Photo overleaf →

Chocolate hazelnut brownies

My go-to, quick and easy crowd-pleaser of a brownie. I slightly undercook mine as I love the gooey centre but it's personal preference. I could eat these every day, no problem, but then again I am known to eat peanut butter straight from the jar! Slightly warmed the brownies double up beautifully as a pudding with a huge scoop of vanilla ice cream.

Makes 9 squares
—

250g crunchy peanut butter (I like peanut butter that doesn't contain palm oil)
175g dark chocolate (minimum 70% cocoa solids)
275g dark soft brown sugar
25g unsalted butter
3 eggs
100g self-raising flour
75g chocolate-hazelnut spread

Topping:
75g blanched hazelnuts, chopped
50g dark chocolate (minimum 70% cocoa solids)

Preheat the oven to 160°C fan (180°C/350°F/Gas Mark 4). Grease a 20cm square baking tin with fairly high sides and line the base with greaseproof paper.

Put 200g of the peanut butter, the chocolate, sugar and butter into a medium-sized saucepan over a low/medium heat and stir until everything is mixed together and the sugar has almost completely dissolved.

Remove from the heat and allow to cool slightly, then add the eggs one at a time, mixing well in between each addition. The mix will be glossy after the eggs have been added. Sift the flour over the chocolate mix and stir in. Pour the brownie mixture into the prepared tin.

Heat the remaining 50g peanut butter in a small pan until warm and runny, then drizzle over the brownie mix. Dot the chocolate-hazelnut spread on top. Using a sharp knife, swirl the top to make lovely swirls of peanut butter and chocolate spread.

Bake for about 25 minutes – I like my brownies extra gooey (bake a bit longer if you want them to be more cake-like). Remove from the oven and allow to cool.

Meanwhile, spread the chopped hazelnuts on a small baking tray and toast in the oven for about 5 minutes until golden. Remove and set aside.

Once the brownie has cooled, melt the chocolate for the topping either in the microwave, in 30-second bursts, or in a heatproof bowl set over a saucepan of boiling water. Drizzle the melted chocolate in lines across the brownie, then sprinkle on the toasted hazelnuts.

Cut into squares and enjoy, or warm in the microwave, on 20-second bursts, and eat as a pudding with ice cream.

Apricot, apple & cashew flapjacks

Flapjacks are the ideal on-the-go snack. The ones here are full of oats, dried fruit and nuts, which all serve well to give you a little energy boost when needed. I much prefer a chewy flapjack to a crunchy one but it's really personal preference. Enjoy the sweet softness of the apple as a lovely little surprise versus the crunchy almost milky cashews.

Swap the nuts and dried fruit around to your preference — you can even add some desiccated coconut or chocolate chips if you are feeling naughty!

Makes 10 rectangles

—

100g cashews
50g light soft brown sugar
pinch of salt
150g unsalted butter
70g golden syrup
100g dried apricots
1 eating apple, peeled and
   cored
200g rolled oats
pinch of ground cinnamon

Preheat the oven to 140°C fan (160°C/325°F/Gas Mark 3). Line a 25cm square cake tin.

Put the cashews in a dry frying pan and toast over a medium heat for about 10 minutes until golden brown. Set aside.

Combine the sugar, salt, butter and syrup in a large saucepan. Set over a low heat and melt together, stirring occasionally. When the mixture starts to bubble, remove from the heat.

Roughly chop the toasted cashews, dried apricots and apple.

Add the rolled oats to the syrup mixture, then stir in the cashews, apricots and apple. Tip the mixture into the prepared tin and push into the corners, gently pressing to level. Sprinkle over the cinnamon.

Bake for 30–35 minutes until golden, or a little longer if you prefer flapjacks to be a little crunchier.

Remove from the oven and allow to cool slightly before cutting into 10 rectangles. Store in an airtight container.

Cranberry, orange & hazelnut biscotti

I used to bake biscotti and wrap them up in cellophane, tied with brown twine, to give as gifts to people I worked with at school. I think a little home-made present like this is really lovely and it always went down a treat with tired teachers! These are fab in a trifle too.

Makes about 30
—

100g skinned hazelnuts, roughly chopped
300g plain flour, plus extra for dusting
100g golden caster sugar
100g light soft brown sugar
1 tsp baking powder
grated zest of 1 orange
100g dried cranberries
2 eggs
splash of milk, if needed
100g white chocolate (optional)

Preheat the oven to 180°C fan (200°C/400°F/Gas Mark 6). Line two baking sheets with greaseproof paper.

Spread out the hazelnuts in a small baking tray and toast in the oven for 10 minutes.

Meanwhile, mix together the flour, both types of sugar, the baking powder, orange zest and dried cranberries in a bowl.

Add the toasted hazelnuts. Make a well in the centre of the mix and crack in the eggs. Mix together with your hands, drawing the dry ingredients into the eggs, and knead together to make a soft dough. If the dough is too dry to come together, add a splash of milk.

Turn out on to a floured work surface and divide into two equal pieces. Using your hands, roll each piece into a sausage shape.

Place one shaped piece of dough on each baking sheet and flatten slightly. Bake for 20–25 minutes until golden and firm to the touch.

Remove from the oven and reduce the oven temperature to 140°C fan (160°F/325°F/Gas Mark 3). Allow the biscuit 'sausages' to cool slightly, then use a sharp bread knife to cut them across, on a slight diagonal, into 1cm-thick slices.

Lay the slices flat on the lined baking sheets and return to the oven to bake for 15–20 minutes until crisp, turning the biscotti over once halfway through. Transfer the biscotti to a wire rack and allow to cool fully.

If decorating with white chocolate, melt it in a heatproof bowl set over a pan of simmering water. Either dip one end of the biscotti into the chocolate or drizzle it over one half. Leave to set on greaseproof paper.

Enjoy with a big cup of coffee or hot chocolate.

Chewy chocolate orange cookies

Terry's Chocolate Oranges remind me of Christmas. When we were children, we always got one in our stocking. I would eat all the segments first and then the core, which was the best bit! A couple of Christmases ago, Dennis (my Pug) managed to open the Terry's box and remove a single chocolate segment. Luckily he wasn't ill but he looked pretty pleased with himself. Chocolate and orange go together like pie and mash or fish and chips, but the subtle addition of cardamom brings these lovely soft and chewy cookies right up to date.

Makes about 30
—

10 cardamom pods
grated zest of 1 orange
250g unsalted butter, softened
200g light soft brown sugar
200g dark soft brown sugar
2 large eggs
320g plain flour
50g cocoa powder
1 tsp baking powder
pinch of salt
1 Terry's Milk Chocolate Orange (about 175g)
150g dark chocolate (minimum 70% cocoa solids)

Preheat the oven to 160°C fan (180°C/350°F/Gas Mark 4). Line two large baking sheets with greaseproof paper.

Using a pestle and mortar, lightly crush the cardamom pods so you can extract the seeds. Remove and discard all the shells/husks. Add the orange zest to the seeds and smash this all up together until combined.

Tip into a large mixing bowl and add the butter and both types of sugar. Using an electric mixer, cream together until fluffy – this will take a few minutes.

Add the eggs one at a time, mixing well between each egg. If the mixture starts to curdle add a spoonful of the flour. Sift the flour, cocoa powder, baking powder and salt into the bowl and mix until combined.

Chop up both types of chocolate into chunks and fold them through the mix.

Bake the cookies in batches (cool and reline the baking sheets before using again). Drop the mix in heaped tablespoonfuls on to the lined baking sheets (don't flatten the heaps). Bake for 10–12 minutes (10 minutes gives you super-gooey cookies, 12 minutes they will be a bit firmer).

Allow to cool on the baking sheets for a couple of minutes before transferring carefully to a wire rack to finish cooling.

Serve with a huge scoop of ice cream, or keep a cookie (wrapped up) in your handbag for emergencies!

Macadamia nut & raspberry jam biscuits

A grown-up jammy dodger – that's what this is! The addition of Amaretto makes the biscuits strictly for adults only, so if you are making them for children just leave out the alcohol. You can be creative with the shapes. These are fab biscuits for seasonal gifts – just change the shape and use fruit that is in season for the jam.

Makes about 10

—

Jam:
200g raspberries
150g golden caster sugar
splash of Amaretto liqueur
grated zest of 1 lemon
juice of ½ lemon

First make the jam. Place a small plate in the freezer. Put the raspberries, sugar, Amaretto, lemon zest and juice in a saucepan and stir over a low heat until the sugar has dissolved. Turn the heat up and bubble for 15 minutes, stirring occasionally.

Now test the jam to see if it will set. Take the plate out of the freezer and remove the pan from the heat. Drop a small amount of the hot jam on the plate and wait a few seconds, then run your finger through the jam. If the surface wrinkles the jam is ready. If the jam isn't ready, return to the heat and boil for a further 5 minutes, then repeat the testing process. Allow the jam to cool.

For the shortbread, preheat the oven to 160°C fan (180°C/350°F/Gas Mark 4). Spread out the macadamia nuts on a baking tray and lightly toast in the oven for about 5 minutes. Set aside to cool. Leave the oven on.

Put the soft butter and both types of sugar in a large bowl and beat with an electric mixer until light and pale. Add the egg yolk, flour, ground almonds, macadamia nuts, lemon zest and salt to the bowl and mix in briefly. Get your hands in and bring the mixture together into a ball of dough that will leave the sides of the bowl cleanly. Do not overwork the dough or handle it too much. Flatten into a disc and wrap in cling film, then chill for 30 minutes.

Don't handle the biscuit mix too much as this will make it tough!

Shortbread:
50g macadamia nuts, chopped
100g unsalted butter, softened
25g light soft brown sugar
25g golden caster sugar
1 egg yolk
120g plain flour, plus extra for dusting
15g ground almonds
finely grated zest of 1 lemon
¼ tsp salt

Lightly dust the work surface and rolling pin with flour. Roll out the shortbread dough to about 3mm thickness. Cut out about twenty 5 x 5cm squares, ideally using a biscuit cutter. In half of them cut out a smaller square in the middle – these will be the top biscuits of the sandwiches.

Place all the biscuits, in one layer, on a baking sheet lined with greaseproof paper. Return to the fridge to firm up for about 15 minutes.

Bake for 12– 15 minutes until golden brown. Remove from the oven. If the shapes have spread you can neaten them up by immediately trimming the edges with the cutter. Transfer carefully to a wire rack and allow to cool.

Once the biscuits are cold, drop a teaspoonful of the cooled jam into the centre of each whole square. Place a cut-out square on top – you should be able to see the raspberry jam through the centre of the top shortbread. Sprinkle with sifted icing sugar. Stored in an airtight tin these should keep for a few days.

Photo overleaf →

* If you're watching
salt levels or baking
for children then
leave out the salt
in the caramel

Millionaire shortbread hearts

This is my take on the millionaire shortbread. It's a little daintier and, as I'm a romantic, they are heart shaped! I used to bake these and package them in glass Kilner jars with brown string to give as gifts.

Makes about 15

—

Caramel:
120g unsalted butter
120g light brown muscovado sugar
100ml double cream
½ tsp rock salt

Shortbread:
85g golden caster sugar
170g unsalted butter, softened
230g plain flour, plus extra for dusting
25g ground almonds
pinch of salt

Topping:
150g dark chocolate (minimum 70% cocoa solids)
50g good-quality white chocolate
toasted flaked almonds

For the caramel, melt the butter with the brown sugar in a large saucepan over a medium heat, swirling the mixture in the pan to prevent sticking. When the sugar has dissolved, allow the mixture to bubble and froth until it turns to a golden caramel colour. Remove from the heat, pour in the double cream and whisk thoroughly until thick and smooth. Sprinkle with the salt. Transfer to a bowl and place in the fridge to cool and thicken.

To make the shortbread, beat together the sugar and butter until pale and fluffy. Add the flour, ground almonds and salt and mix together briefly with your hands – do not overwork the dough. Wrap in cling film and chill for about 30 minutes.

Preheat the oven to 160°C fan (180°C/350°F/Gas Mark 4). Line two baking sheets with greaseproof paper.

Roll out the shortbread dough on a lightly floured work surface to about 3mm thick. Cut out heart shapes 5–6cm across the top and place on the lined baking sheet. Re-roll the dough trimmings and continue to cut out heart shapes until the dough is used up. Return to the fridge to firm up for 20 minutes.

Bake for 15–18 minutes until lightly golden and set. Keep an eye on the shortbread during baking to ensure that the edges do not catch.

Remove from the oven. If the heart shapes have spread a bit, you can trim the edges using the cutter again, but you need to be quick before the biscuits set. Allow to cool for a couple of minutes before transferring to a wire rack to finish cooling.

Turn over half of the heart biscuits and dollop a teaspoonful of the thick caramel on to the centre of each base. Set a second heart on top, right way up, and press down lightly. Place the sandwich biscuits in one layer on a flat tray lined with greaseproof paper.

Melt the dark chocolate in a heatproof bowl set over a saucepan of simmering water. Drizzle the dark chocolate across each heart sandwich biscuit. Melt the white chocolate, then drizzle this lightly over the top of the dark chocolate. Before the chocolate sets, sprinkle toasted flaked almonds on to the chocolate so they stick. Leave to set in a cool place.

Granola

This is great as a snack or sprinkled on top of my Chocolate and Banana Waffles (page 146). Or, you could use it as an alternative to a crumble topping. There is no refined sugar in this recipe – maple syrup, honey and dates add the sweetness – and my beloved coconut oil makes an appearance. As far as granola goes this is luxury, high-end and full of flavour, but not completely naughty. So go ahead and have some sprinkled on your fruit and yoghurt at breakfast.

Makes about 500g

—

2 tbsp melted coconut oil
120ml maple syrup
2 tbsp honey
1 tsp vanilla bean paste
250g rolled oats
1/2 tsp ground cinnamon
50g flaked almonds
50g whole blanched
    almonds
50g hazelnuts
150g mixed seeds
    (pumpkin, sesame,
    sunflower)
50g desiccated coconut
25g flaked coconut
100g stoneless dates,
    chopped

Preheat the oven to 130°C fan (150°C/300°F/Gas Mark 2). Line a baking tray with greaseproof paper.

In a bowl mix together the coconut oil, maple syrup, honey and vanilla. Add the oats, cinnamon, flaked almonds, whole almonds, hazelnuts and mixed seeds.

Tip on to the lined baking tray and spread out. Bake for 20 minutes (stir around once halfway through).

Add the desiccated and flaked coconut, then stir through the chopped dates. Bake for a further 15–20 minutes, stirring twice during the cooking time.

Remove from the oven and tip on to a clean sheet of greaseproof paper to cool. Store in an airtight container.

Coconut Layers

My Mam says that when she was pregnant with me she ate so many Bounty bars she was surprised I didn't come out looking like a coconut! My sister, Tanya, also had this obsession, which now seems to have been passed on to me – I love anything coconut-flavoured and I can't get enough of coconut oil. These squares should keep most coconutty lovers happy!

Makes 12 squares

—

130ml coconut oil, melted, plus extra for greasing
200g dark soft brown sugar
3 eggs
30g good-quality cocoa powder
100g dark chocolate (minimum 70% cocoa solids), chopped into small pieces
140ml boiling water
85g plain flour
40g ground almonds
½ tsp bicarbonate of soda
pinch of salt

Coconut Layer:
250g full-fat soft cheese
200ml double cream
1 tsp vanilla bean paste
200g desiccated coconut

Ganache:
300ml double cream
150g dark chocolate (minimum 70% cocoa solids), chopped into small pieces
1 Bounty bar, chopped

Preheat the oven to 160°C fan (180°C/350°F/Gas Mark 4). Lightly grease a 25cm square cake tin and line with greaseproof paper.

Put the coconut oil, sugar and eggs in a mixing bowl. Beat with an electric mixer on a medium speed for 3 minutes.

In a measuring jug, combine the cocoa powder, chocolate and boiling water and stir until the chocolate has melted. Pour the chocolate mixture into the egg and sugar mix in a steady stream while beating on a low speed. Add the flour, ground almonds, bicarbonate of soda and salt and mix in with a spatula. The mixture will be very runny but this is fine.

Pour the mixture into the prepared tin. Bake for 25–30 minutes until just set and a skewer inserted into the middle comes out clean except for a few crumbs. Cool in the tin.

For the coconut layer, whisk together the soft cheese, double cream and vanilla in a bowl, then mix in the coconut. Tip the coconut mix over the cooled chocolate base. Spread out evenly.

To make the ganache topping, heat the cream in a saucepan until bubbles start appearing on the surface. Put the chocolate in a bowl. Pour the warm cream over the chocolate and leave for about 10 minutes, then stir until combined and smooth.

Pour the ganache evenly over the coconut layer and top with the chopped Bounty bar. Allow to set before cutting into squares.

Piña colada macaroons

In my opinion these untidy, jaggedy mounds of coconut goodness put the much more delicate and dainty macarons firmly in the shade! The dried pineapple and coconut really make these macaroons taste like piña colada cocktails but without the artificial flavours that you sometimes get. Of course, the rum helps!

Makes 18—20

—

200g unsweetened
    desiccated coconut
150g flaked coconut
100g dried pineapple,
    finely chopped
450g condensed milk
1 tsp vanilla bean paste
grated zest of 1 lime
2 tsp white rum
4 egg whites

To decorate:
200g white chocolate
1 tsp white rum
dried pineapple quarters
glacé cherries, cut in half

Preheat the oven to 160°C fan (180°C/350°F/Gas Mark 4). Line a baking sheet with greaseproof paper.

In a bowl mix together the desiccated and flaked coconut and the dried pineapple. Pour over the condensed milk and add the vanilla bean paste, lime zest and rum. Mix together.

In a separate bowl whisk the egg whites until they form soft, fluffy peaks. Add the egg whites to the coconut mixture and fold together gently using a spatula until all the ingredients are evenly distributed.

Using a dessertspoon, spoon mounds of the mixture on to the lined baking sheet. Do not flatten them – they should stand tall and stick out like crazy hay bales!

Bake for 12–15 minutes until the sticky-out bits have turned golden brown and the macaroons are just set on the outside (they should still be soft in the middle). Transfer to a wire rack to cool.

Soften the white chocolate with the rum in a heatproof bowl set over a saucepan of simmering water. Remove from the heat and stir until smooth and runny.

Drizzle the chocolate back and forth over the macaroons, then stick one of the pineapple quarters and a cherry half on top of each. Leave to set.

Take a bite, close your eyes and pretend you are on the beach!

Photo overleaf →

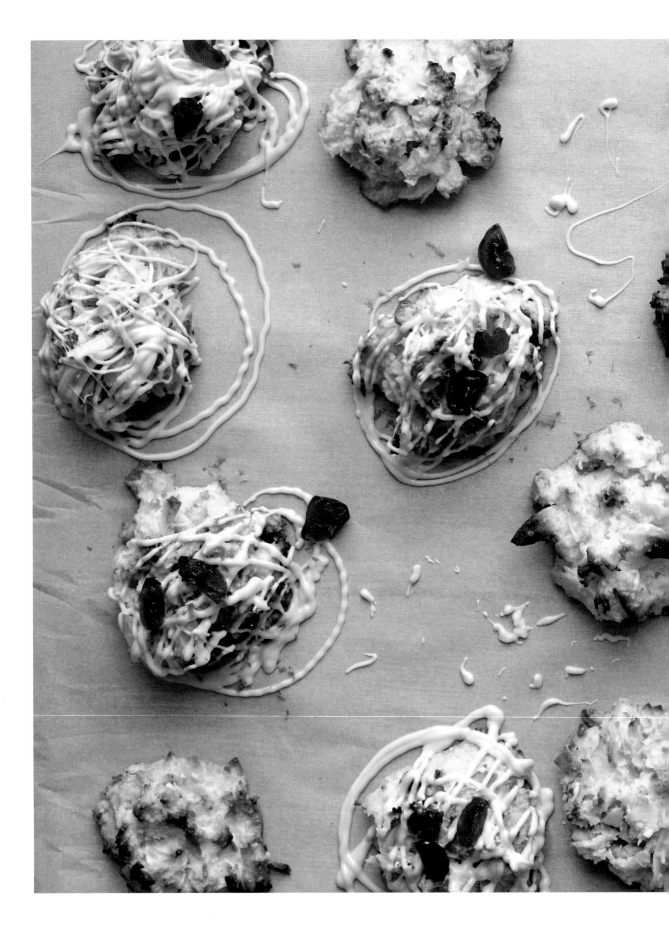

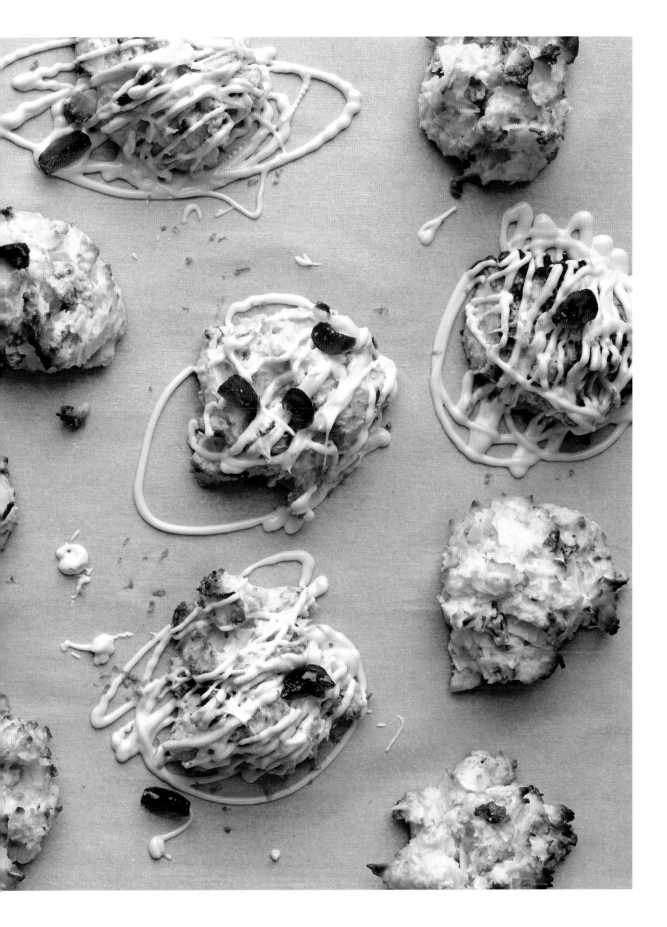

This chapter was such fun to write – I love making pastry, and there are so many different types, from puff and choux to shortcrust and flaky (which isn't as tricky as you might think…). And if you make a larger quantity, you can use what you need and freeze the rest.

—

Whatever type of pastry you are making, use really good-quality butter. I like Normandy butter as it has such a good flavour and doesn't melt as fast as cheaper butters. I have a real passion for France and anything French, and I feel pastries have a lot to do with this. I'd happily scoff pastries for breakfast every day accompanied with a big bowl of chocolat au lait.

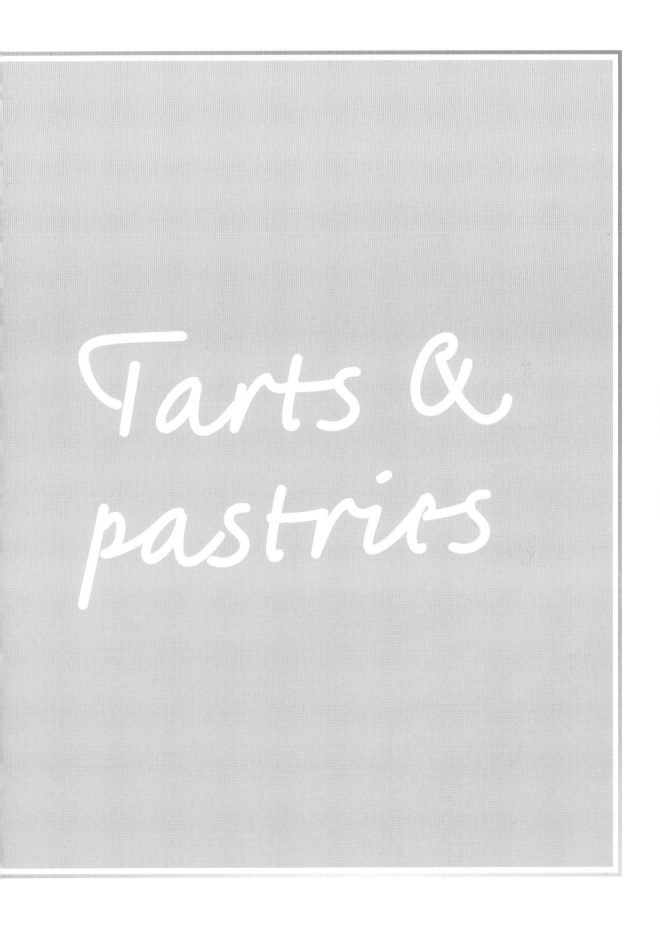

Tarts &
pastries

Cherry Amaretto Bakewell tart

A great Bakewell tart can bring a tear to my eye, simply for the memories it holds for me of my Nan. She made the BEST Bakewell tart. I remember watching her make the pastry – she'd let me make little jam tarts with the cut-offs – then delicately spreading jam in the pastry case and filling it to the brim with the sweet almond mix. We had to try to keep my Grandad from helping himself before it had even cooled! My addition of Amaretto to the thick cherry jam and the almond filling gives it that little extra something.

Serves 8

—

Pâte sucrée:
100g golden caster sugar
100g unsalted butter
4 egg yolks
175g plain flour,
    plus extra for dusting
25g ground almonds
pinch of salt

Jam:
200g frozen cherries
100g golden caster sugar
2 tbsp Amaretto liqueur
grated zest of 1 lemon

Filling:
120g unsalted butter,
    softened
120g golden caster sugar
1 tbsp Amaretto liqueur
2 eggs
120g ground almonds
pinch of salt
finely grated zest of
    1 lemon
1 tbsp plain flour
30g flaked almonds

Preheat the oven to 160°C fan (180°C/350°F/Gas Mark 4).

For the pâte sucrée, beat together the sugar and butter in a large bowl with an electric mixer until pale and fluffy. Beat in the egg yolks followed by the flour, ground almonds and salt. Bring together with your hands to form a ball of dough. Flatten this slightly, then wrap in cling film and chill for 30 minutes.

Roll out the pastry on a floured work surface to 3–4mm thick. Lift with a rolling pin and drape into a 23cm loose-bottomed fluted tart tin. Gently press the pastry into the flutes and tease in the edges. Remove the excess pastry so it is just at the top of the tin. Prick the base of the pastry case with a fork.

Scrunch up a piece of greaseproof paper, then spread out and use to line the pastry case. Fill with baking beans. Bake blind for 15 minutes, then remove the paper and baking beans and bake for a further 5–10 minutes until set and golden. Set aside to cool. Leave the oven on but increase the temperature to 170°C fan (190°C/375°F/Gas Mark 5).

Next make the jam. Place a side plate in the freezer. Put the frozen cherries, sugar, Amaretto and lemon zest in a small saucepan. Set over a low heat and stir to dissolve the sugar. Turn up the heat and allow to bubble away for about 10 minutes, stirring occasionally, then test the jam for set. Remove the pan from the heat and spoon a blob of hot jam on to the frozen plate. Leave for a few seconds, then run your finger through the jam – if the surface wrinkles, the jam is ready. If it doesn't, return to the heat and bubble for a further 5 minutes, then test again. Allow to cool.

For the filling, beat together the butter and sugar in a large bowl with an electric mixer until fluffy. Add the Amaretto and eggs, then mix in the ground almonds, salt, lemon zest and flour.

Spread the cherry jam evenly in the baked pastry case. Top with the almond filling and level out with a spatula. Sprinkle the flaked almonds over the filling. Bake for 35–40 minutes until the filling is just set and the almonds look toasted and golden. Cool before serving.

Croissants

Simply served warm from the oven – torn in half and dipped into a bowl of rich hot chocolate – is my favourite way to enjoy these croissants. They do take a bit of time and effort but you will be so chuffed with yourself when you taste the outcome.

Makes about 24
—

500g strong white bread flour, plus extra for dusting
10g instant yeast
10g salt
50g golden caster sugar
100ml lukewarm whole milk
200ml cold water
250g cold unsalted butter

Egg wash:
1 egg
splash of milk

Sift the flour into the large bowl of a free-standing electric mixer fitted with a dough hook. Make a well in the middle. On one side add the yeast and on the opposite side add the salt and sugar. Pour in the milk and 150ml of the water. Mix on a low speed for 2 minutes until all the flour has been incorporated (add more water, a little at a time, if the mix is looking too dry), then turn up the speed to medium and mix/knead for 5–6 minutes to make a smooth, stretchy dough.

Tip the dough out on to a lightly floured work surface and shape into a smooth ball. Place in a plastic bag and leave to rest in the fridge for about 2 hours.

Put the butter between two pieces of greaseproof paper and bash/roll out to a 20 x 30cm rectangle that is about 5mm thick. Return to the fridge to chill for 30 minutes.

Flour the work surface again, then roll out the dough away from you into a rectangle about 30 x 50cm. Lay the butter rectangle on the bottom two-thirds of the dough rectangle. Fold the top section of dough (without butter) down over the top half of the butter rectangle. Now fold up the bottom third of butter-covered dough. You should now have stacked layers of dough, butter, dough, butter, dough. Pinch the edges so the butter is inside. Place in a plastic bag and chill in the fridge for 30 minutes.

Place the dough on the floured surface so a short side is nearest to you. Roll out away from you into a rectangle again. Fold up the bottom third, then fold down the top third. Pinch the edges together. Put into the plastic bag and chill for 30 minutes.

Repeat this rolling and folding process (called a 'turn') three more times, chilling in between for 30 minutes. This will make a total of four turns. Put the dough back in the plastic bag and leave in the fridge for at least 8 hours, but preferably overnight.

Line two baking sheets with greaseproof paper.

*Try this: just before rolling the triangles up place ½ teaspoon of crunchy peanut butter and ½ teaspoon of jam onto the wide end, then roll up for a really naughty treat. Or, if that's not your thing, try salted caramel or a square of chocolate.

Lightly flour the work surface again and roll out the well-chilled dough to a rectangle about 6–7mm thick. Trim the edges so it is neat and even. Cut the piece of dough in half lengthways so you have two long strips. Cut the two strips into triangles.

To shape each croissant, start at the wide end of the triangle and roll up towards the point while gently holding the point in place. Carefully lift up the rolled-up shape and place on a lined baking sheet. Curl the ends in so they nearly meet. Repeat with all the triangles, leaving space in between them on the baking sheets.

Put the sheets into clean plastic bags and leave the shaped croissants in a warm place to rise for 1–2 hours until doubled in size.

Preheat the oven to 180°C fan (200°C/400°F/Gas Mark 6).

Lightly beat the egg with the milk using a fork to make the egg wash.

Remove the baking sheets from the bags and gently brush each risen croissant with the egg wash. Bake for 15–20 minutes until crisp and golden. Transfer to a wire rack to cool slightly.

Serve warm with jam and enjoy with a cup of coffee or dip into a bowl of hot chocolate.

* If you don't like coconut, you can leave
it out or swap for chopped nuts.
Lemon curd would also work
instead of jam.

Cornflake tart

For me, this is the ultimate school dinner pudding, served warm drenched in custard. Two of my oldest friends love this and request it frequently! I think it's the nostalgic memories it brings back – and it being completely delicious! Just don't scrimp on the slice size or custard!

Serves 8

—

Pastry:

150g plain flour, plus extra for dusting
25g ground almonds
pinch of salt
100g cold unsalted butter, cubed
30g golden caster sugar
finely grated zest of 1 lemon
1 large egg yolk

Filling:

75g unsalted butter
150g golden syrup
50g light soft brown sugar
pinch of salt
150g cornflakes
25g desiccated coconut
100g raspberry/ strawberry/cherry jam (preferably home-made – see my recipe for Jam Jam Jam on page 152)

To make the pastry, put the flour, ground almonds and salt into a large bowl. Add the butter and rub in to make a breadcrumb texture. Add the sugar and lemon zest and mix through with a blunt knife, then add the egg yolk and continue mixing with the knife. If the pastry dough isn't quite coming together, add a little cold water, a teaspoon at a time.

Now use your hands to bring the pastry dough together without kneading it too much. Flatten into a disc and wrap in cling film, then chill in the fridge for 1–2 hours.

Preheat the oven to 180°C fan (200°C/400°F/Gas Mark 6).

Roll out the chilled pastry on a lightly floured work surface to about 3mm thick. Use the rolling pin to lift the pastry up and into a 23cm fluted, loose-bottomed flan tin. Take a small piece of excess pastry dough from the edge and use it to push the pastry into the flutes of the tin. Trim off all the excess pastry. Prick the base of the pastry case with a fork, then chill for 15 minutes.

Scrunch up a piece of greaseproof paper, then smooth it out and use to line the pastry case. Fill with baking beans. Blind bake for 20 minutes, then remove the paper and beans and bake for a further 10 minutes until golden brown. Remove from the oven, but leave the oven on.

Combine the butter, syrup, sugar and salt in a saucepan set over a low/medium heat and allow to melt together and become glossy and thick, stirring occasionally. Remove from the heat, then tip in the cornflakes and coconut and mix in gently to cover evenly in the hot syrup – try not to break up the cornflakes too much.

Spread your home-made jam over the bottom of the cooked pastry case and top with the cornflake mixture. Return the tart to the oven to bake for 15–20 minutes until the filling is golden brown.

Serve warm with Vanilla Custard (page 121).

Berry crème tarts

Like beautiful shiny gems resting on a cushion of vanilla crème, these look impressive but are actually fairly easy to make. Change the fruits to suit the seasons or your preferences, or add some chocolate and nuts for a different variation. If you're making the tarts for children, just leave out the Amaretto.

Makes 8
—

Pastry:
100g unsalted butter, softened
100g golden caster sugar
3 large egg yolks
200g plain flour, plus extra for dusting
pinch of salt
50g ground almonds
grated zest of 1 lemon
beaten egg, for egg wash

Crème pâtissière:
300ml whole milk
75ml single cream
1 tsp vanilla bean paste
75g golden caster sugar
3 medium egg yolks
30g cornflour
40g unsalted butter, in small pieces

Decoration:
200g strawberries
200g blueberries
200g redcurrants
2 tbsp apricot preserve or jam
25ml Amaretto liqueur

First make the pastry. Put the butter and sugar in a bowl and beat with an electric mixer until fluffy. Add the egg yolks and beat in. Add the flour, salt, ground almonds and lemon zest and mix to a dough. Knead lightly together. Wrap and chill for about 20 minutes.

Preheat the oven to 160°C fan (180°C/350°F/Gas Mark 4).

Roll out the dough on a lightly floured work surface to about 3mm thick. Cut out eight rounds and lay each in a 4–5cm diameter fluted tart tin. Press neatly into the flutes. Line the pastry cases with greaseproof paper and fill with baking beans. Bake blind for 15 minutes.

Remove the paper and beans, then brush the pastry cases with egg wash. Return to the oven and bake for a further 5 minutes until golden. Set aside to cool.

For the crème pâtissière, put the milk, cream and vanilla in a large, heavy-based saucepan and bring to the boil. While this is heating up, mix together the sugar, egg yolks and cornflour in a large bowl until smooth.

Once the milk mixture has come to the boil, remove from the heat and pour about a quarter of it into the eggs and sugar. Whisk together, then whisk this mixture into the hot milk remaining in the saucepan. Set over a low/medium heat and keep whisking until the mixture thickens. Remove from the heat. Add the butter and stir through until melted. Place a piece of greaseproof paper on top of the crème pâtissière to prevent a skin from forming. Allow to cool, then chill for at least 1 hour.

Slice the strawberries and layer in the bottom of the pastry cases.

Spoon the cooled and thickened crème pâtissière into a piping bag and snip a 1cm hole in the end. Starting just inside the rim of each pastry case, pipe crème pâtissière in swirls, building up to a higher centre. Add the blueberries in two concentric rings around the edge and lay a bunch of redcurrants on the middle.

Gently heat the apricot preserve in a small bowl in the microwave until runny, then stir through the Amaretto. Brush this glaze over the fruit and edge of the pastry case. Leave to set before serving (these need to be eaten fairly soon after making, otherwise the pastry will go soft).

Back-to-front chocolate & pear profiteroles

These are really just profiteroles, only they are filled back to front!
Dark chocolate and pear is such a lovely combination I thought it would
work well on something as delicate as a profiterole roll: light and crisp
choux against the soft pear and rich chocolate, with the little surprise
of the cream on top! Of course if you are a stickler for rules then put
the chocolate on top and the cream in the middle. That's fine too.

Serves 4

Choux:
55g unsalted butter
1 tsp vanilla bean paste
75g plain flour
½ tsp ground cinnamon
pinch of salt
2 eggs

Filling:
3 pears, peeled, cored
  and chopped
1 star anise
1 cinnamon stick, broken
300ml double cream
150g dark chocolate
  (minimum 70% cocoa
  solids), broken into
  pieces

Topping:
300ml double cream
25g toasted flaked
  almonds

Preheat the oven to 190°C fan (210°C/420°F/Gas Mark 6/7).
Line two baking sheets with greaseproof paper.

Put the butter, vanilla and 160ml water in a large saucepan over a
medium heat and allow the butter to melt, then bring to the boil.

Meanwhile, sift the flour, cinnamon and salt on to a folded piece of
greaseproof paper.

When the buttery water is at boiling point, remove from the heat and
in one go drop the flour into the water. Mix vigorously with a wooden
spoon until the mixture leaves the sides of the pan and forms a soft
ball in the centre. Return to a low heat and continue to stir the balled
mixture for about 1 minute.

Transfer the hot mix to a bowl and stir round a little to help it cool
down. When the mixture has cooled slightly, add one egg and beat
using a handheld electric mixer until the egg is incorporated and the
mixture is starting to look thick and glossy. (It may look like it is curdling
but keep beating and it will come together.)

Add the second egg and beat again until the choux dough is smooth,
thick and glossy. It should drop off a spoon slowly and hold its shape.

Spoon the dough into a piping bag and snip a 2cm opening in the end.
Pipe out 4cm rounds on the lined baking sheets, leaving a little space
between each one.

Bake for 25–30 minutes until golden, risen and crisp. Remove from
the oven and transfer the choux profiteroles to a wire rack to cool.

You can make the profiteroles ahead and freeze them as soon as they have cooled. To defrost and reheat, put them in an oven preheated to 180°C fan (200°C/400°F/Gas Mark 6) for 5 minutes to crisp up.

For the filling, combine the chopped pears, star anise and cinnamon stick in a small saucepan and cook over a low heat until the pear has softened and is infused with the spices. Allow to cool, then remove the star anise and cinnamon stick and blitz in a food processor to a thick purée.

Heat the cream in a small saucepan until it just starts to boil. Remove from the heat, add the dark chocolate and leave for 10 minutes before stirring together to make a ganache.

Whip up the double cream for the topping in a large bowl until just thick and smooth.

Slice the choux buns in half. Spoon the chocolate ganache into a piping bag and snip a 1cm opening in the end. Put the whipped cream into a second piping bag fitted with a nozzle of your choice.

Pipe ganache into the bottom half of each profiterole and top with a dollop of pear purée. Set the top half of the profiterole in place and pipe on a swirl of whipped cream.

Roughly chop the toasted flaked almonds and sprinkle on top of the cream.

Photo overleaf →

Almond & pear pinwheel pastries

I just love pastry, in any shape or form, but Danish pastries are one of my favourites. The almost bread-like texture in the middle of these pinwheels is the best part – I always pick one that is slightly undercooked in the middle for that stodgy goodness! Pear and almond is a classic combination and the little drizzle of maple syrup makes these extra special.

Makes 12–15
—
Danish pastry dough:
500g strong white bread flour, plus extra for sprinkling
10g instant yeast
10g salt
50g golden caster sugar
2 eggs
200ml lukewarm whole milk
250g cold unsalted butter

Filling/topping:
50g unsalted butter, softened
50g golden caster sugar
1 egg
50g ground almonds
1/2 tsp almond extract
1 large ripe pear
50g flaked almonds
beaten egg for egg wash
maple syrup
apricot preserve or jam

Sift the flour into the large bowl of a free-standing electric mixer fitted with dough hook. On one side add the yeast and on the opposite side add the salt and sugar. Add the eggs and the milk. Mix on a low speed for 2 minutes, then turn up the speed to medium and mix/knead for 5–6 minutes to make a smooth, stretchy dough.

Tip the dough out on to a lightly floured work surface and shape into a smooth ball. Place in a plastic bag and leave to rest in the fridge for about 1 hour.

Meanwhile, put the butter between two pieces of greaseproof paper and bash/roll out to a 15 x 20cm rectangle that is about 5mm thick.

Flour the work surface again, then roll out the dough away from you into a rectangle about 20 x 35cm. Lay the butter rectangle on the bottom two-thirds of the dough rectangle. Fold the top section of dough (without butter) down over the top half of the butter rectangle. Now fold up the bottom third of butter-covered dough. You should now have stacked layers of dough, butter, dough, butter, dough. Pinch the edges so the butter is inside. Place in a plastic bag and chill in the fridge for 30 minutes.

Place the dough on the floured surface so a short side is nearest to you. Roll out away from you into a rectangle again. Fold up the bottom third, then fold down the top third. Put into the plastic bag and chill for 30 minutes.

Repeat this rolling and folding process (called a 'turn') twice, chilling in between for 30 minutes. This will make a total of three turns. Put the dough back in the plastic bag and leave in the fridge for at least 8 hours but preferably overnight.

Cut the dough in half. Keep one piece, wrapped in the fridge, for the Cheese and Mushroom Danish Rounds (page 108), or freeze to make more pinwheel pastries another time (thaw before using).

Roll out the other piece on a lightly floured surface to a rectangle about 3mm thick, turning the sheet of dough as you roll so it doesn't spring back. Trim the edges using a sharp knife, then cut out 8cm squares – you should be able to cut 12–15 squares.

To shape each square, make a 2cm cut in each corner diagonally towards the centre, leaving the centre intact. Take the left corner of each triangular cut and fold into the middle, so you end up with four corners in the middle and four flat in a pinwheel shape. Press the middle down firmly with your finger.

Place the pinwheels on a baking sheet lined with greaseproof paper. Put this into a plastic bag and leave to rise in a warm place for 2 hours.

Preheat the oven to 180°C fan (200°C/400°F/Gas Mark 6).

In a small bowl, beat the butter and sugar together until light and fluffy. Add the egg, ground almonds and almond extract, and mix well until combined.

Peel the pear and cut into quarters, removing the core, then cut into pieces about 2mm thick.

Dollop a teaspoon of the almond mix (frangipane) on to the centre of each pinwheel. Lay five to six pieces of pear on top of the pinwheel, slightly overlapping them, then sprinkle with some flaked almonds.

Egg wash the visible dough, then drizzle maple syrup over the pear and almond filling. Bake for 15–20 minutes until golden brown.

Gently heat the apricot preserve until runny. Brush over the pastry for shine. Leave to cool a bit before serving warm, or allow to cool fully.

Photo overleaf →

Cheese & mushroom Danish rounds

I know I've said how much I like sweet Danish pastries, but I love the savoury ones too. These are comforting and cheesy, and I think I prefer them now to sweet ones. In fact, the last couple of times I have made these I haven't had a chance to taste one because my family loves them so much! I like to add mushrooms to most savoury dishes – the earthiness teamed with garlic is one of my favourite flavour combinations and works perfectly in these pastries. They are great for vegetarians but if you want to add bacon or tomato then go for it. Just remember not too much moisture or the pastries could be soggy.

Makes 9

—

½ quantity Danish pastry dough (see Almond and Pear Pinwheel Pastries, page 104), well chilled

Filling:
250g mixed mushrooms (chestnut, mini Portobello, forester, oyster etc), chopped
1 tsp chopped garlic (jarred or fresh)
2 fresh thyme sprigs
knob of butter
olive oil
200g mature Cheddar (or cheese of your choice), grated
beaten egg, for egg wash
salt and freshly ground black pepper

Roll out the dough on a lightly floured surface to a square about 25 x 25cm and about 3mm thick, turning the sheet of dough as you roll so it doesn't spring back. Trim the edges using a sharp knife, then cut out nine 8cm squares.

To shape each pastry, slightly roll over each of the four corners towards the middle and press down, so you have a hexagon/round shape with higher edges. Place the shaped pastries on a baking sheet lined with greaseproof paper and put this into a plastic bag. Leave to rise for 2 hours.

Preheat the oven to 180°C fan (200°C/400°F/Gas Mark 6).

Put the mushrooms in a frying pan with the garlic, thyme, butter and a glug of olive oil. Cook over a medium heat until soft and starting to colour. Season with salt and pepper to taste.

Dollop a spoonful of the mushroom mix in the middle of each pastry and top with grated cheese. Egg wash the visible pastry, then bake for 15–20 minutes until golden brown and the cheese has melted. Serve warm.

Marzipan mince pies

When is too early to get started on the Christmas mince pies? My answer is never! This is a little show-off mince pie recipe that both surprises and delights with the addition of fresh fruit and a sweet almond marzipan. These are wonderful served warm and will definitely get Santa's seal of approval.

Makes 12
—

1 x 411g jar good-quality
  mincemeat
1 apple, peeled, cored
  and finely chopped
1 satsuma, peeled (pith
  removed) and chopped
grated zest of 1 orange
splash of Amaretto
  liqueur

Shortcrust pastry:
150g plain flour
25g ground almonds
pinch of salt
100g cold unsalted butter,
  cut into cubes
30g golden caster sugar
finely grated zest of
  1 lemon
1 large egg yolk
beaten egg, for egg wash
demerara sugar, for
  sprinkling

Marzipan:
100g golden caster sugar
110g icing sugar, plus extra
  for dusting
100g ground almonds
1/2 tsp almond extract
1 egg, beaten

Put the mincemeat, apple, satsuma and orange zest in a bowl and mix together. Add the Amaretto. Cover and leave to soak for 3 hours.

To make the pastry, combine the flour, ground almonds and salt in a large bowl. Add the butter and rub it into the flour with your fingertips until the mixture looks like breadcrumbs. Add the caster sugar and lemon zest and mix in with a table knife, then add the egg yolk and mix together with the knife. If the dough isn't quite coming together, add cold water a teaspoon at a time. Get your hands in and bring the dough together but try not to knead it too much. Shape the dough into a thick disc, wrap in cling film and chill for about an hour.

Preheat the oven to 180°C fan (200°C/400°F/Gas Mark 6).

To make the marzipan, mix both types of sugar and the ground almonds in a large bowl, then rub in the almond extract. Make a well in the middle and tip in the egg. Cut the egg into the dry ingredients using a table knife, to mix together.

Dust a work surface with sifted icing sugar, and knead the marzipan mix briefly to make a smooth paste. Try not to let it get too warm as then the paste can become greasy. Add a bit more icing sugar if the marzipan seems too wet. Shape the marzipan into 12 marble-sized balls and set aside. (Any unused marzipan can be wrapped and stored in the fridge or freezer.)

Flour the work surface, then roll out the chilled pastry to about 3mm thick. Using a plain 9–10cm round cutter, cut out 12 rounds and place them in the holes of a muffin tin (or mince pie tin). Use a star cutter to cut out 12 star shapes that are smaller than the top of the tins.

Stir the mincemeat again, then add a heaped teaspoon into each pastry case. Add a marzipan marble to each, then top with another spoonful of mincemeat, hiding the marzipan. Place the pastry stars on top.

Egg wash the pastry stars, sprinkle them with demerara sugar and bake the pies for 20–25 minutes until the pastry is golden brown. Transfer to a wire rack to cool. Dust with icing sugar and don't forget to keep some for Santa!

Pear & fig tarte tatin

I was actually quite scared the first time I made tarte tatin, I think because it is one of those things you see in fancy restaurants and this always put me off making it. But once I broke it down into its individual elements I found it less daunting. If the thought of making caramel worries you, you can always use a ready-made tinned version – I promise I won't tell anyone! The figs in my tarte tatin add an almost chewy texture and the pecans absorb the juice and become so tasty. You really do need to eat this as soon as it is baked and plated, or you may find the crisp pastry goes a bit soft.

Serves 4
—

Pastry:
150g plain flour, plus extra
   for dusting
150g strong white bread
   flour
pinch of salt
1 tsp ground cinnamon
50g lard, cut into cubes
150ml cold water
200g cold unsalted butter

Filling:
4 ripe pears
4 fresh figs
100g golden caster sugar
50g unsalted butter
50g pecan nuts

Sift both types of flour into a large bowl and stir in the salt and cinnamon. Add the lard and rub in with your fingertips until the mixture looks like breadcrumbs. Stir in the cold water and bring together with your hands to make a dough. Turn out on to a lightly floured surface and knead briefly until smooth. Wrap in cling film and chill for 30 minutes.

Meanwhile, place the cold butter between two pieces of greaseproof paper and bash/roll with a rolling pin until you have a flat 15 x 25cm rectangle that is about 3mm thick.

Roll out the chilled dough on the floured surface (rolling away from you) to a 20 x 40cm rectangle. Lay the butter rectangle on the bottom two-thirds of the dough rectangle. There should be a clear border about 1cm at the bottom and 2.5cm around the sides.

Fold the top, unbuttered third of the dough rectangle down over the middle third, then fold the bottom third up over the middle third (you will now have alternating layers of dough, butter, dough, butter, dough). Pinch the edges together, then wrap and chill for 30 minutes.

Flour the work surface again and set the dough on it so a short side is nearest to you. Roll out away from you into a 20 x 40cm rectangle again. This time fold both the top and bottom of the rectangle in so they meet in the middle, then fold in half like a book. Pinch the edges together. Wrap and chill for 30 minutes.

Roll out the dough into a rectangle as before. Fold the top third down and the bottom third up over it. Wrap and chill for 30 minutes. Repeat this rolling and folding process (called a 'turn') three times, chilling in between for 30 minutes. This will make a total of four turns. Keep the dough in the fridge until ready to use.

You only need half of the pastry for this recipe, so cut the block of pastry in half and wrap one piece in cling film. This can be stored in the freezer for up to one month. Roll out the other piece of pastry on the lightly floured work surface to about the thickness of a £1 coin. Cut out a round that is 5cm bigger than the pan you are going to use (I use an 18cm ovenproof frying pan).

Preheat the oven to 200°C fan (220°C/425°F/Gas Mark 7).

Peel each pear, cut in half lengthways and remove the core using a spoon. Cut the figs in half vertically.

Scatter the sugar in your chosen pan and melt it over a low/medium heat – do not stir but shake the pan every so often to redistribute the sugar. It will liquidise, then start to bubble and turn to a lovely golden-coloured caramel. Add the butter to the caramel and shake the pan gently to mix them together.

Place the pears in the caramel, round-side down, and add the figs cut-side down. Carefully push the pecans into any gaps. Allow to bubble away for about 5 minutes until the pears have started to soften. Remove from the heat.

Carefully lift the pastry round up and over the pan to cover the pear and fig mixture. Using a spatula or wooden spoon, gently tuck the edges of the pastry down inside the edge of the pan so you can no longer see any fruit or caramel.

Poke a small hole in the centre of the pastry lid, then place in the oven to bake for 25–35 minutes until the pastry is golden brown. Remove from the oven and allow to cool in the pan for a couple of minutes.

Place a large inverted plate over the top of the pan and, holding them firmly together, turn over in one swift movement. The tarte tatin should end up on the plate, with the pastry on the bottom. Cool slightly before cutting. Serve with vanilla ice cream.

Do not hesitate when you're flipping over the tarte or the caramel will seep out, and make sure you have an oven glove on each hand/arm to prevent yourself getting burnt.

* With Italian meringue there is no need to bake the assembled pie — the heat of the sugar syrup as you add it to the egg whites 'cooks' them. If you don't have a blowtorch you can place the pie under the grill for 5 minutes to crisp up the meringue peaks.

Peach melba meringue pie

Peach melba always makes me think of the yoghurts I used to eat when I was younger – it took a while for me to realise it was peach and raspberry that made up peach melba! There is no mistaking the two flavours in this summery meringue pie. An ordinary meringue topping can be quite temperamental, but Italian meringue is more stable and reduces the chance of juice being produced during baking. Blowtorching is a bit of a trendy way to crisp up the edges but the pie will look just as good if you don't.

Serves 8

—

Pâte sucrée:
100g golden caster sugar
100g unsalted butter
4 egg yolks
175g plain flour, plus extra
    for dusting
25g ground almonds
grated zest of 1 lemon
pinch of salt
beaten egg, for egg wash

Filling:
6 ripe peaches
1 tbsp light soft brown
    sugar
250g fresh raspberries

Raspberry coulis:
200g fresh raspberries
50g icing sugar
1 tsp lemon juice

Italian meringue:
½ lemon
4 egg whites
200g golden caster sugar
shreds of lemon zest

Preheat the oven to 160°C fan (180°C/350°F/Gas Mark 4).

For the pâte sucrée, beat together the sugar and butter in a large bowl with an electric mixer until pale and fluffy. Beat in the egg yolks followed by the flour, ground almonds, lemon zest and salt. Bring together with your hands to form a ball of dough. Flatten this slightly, then wrap in cling film and chill for 30 minutes.

Roll out the pastry on a floured work surface to 3–4mm thick. Lift with a rolling pin and drape into a 25cm loose-bottomed fluted tart tin. Gently press the pastry into the flutes and tease in the edges. Remove the excess pastry so it is just at the top of the tin. Prick the base of the pastry case with a fork.

Scrunch up a piece of greaseproof paper, then spread out and use to line the pastry case. Fill with baking beans. Bake blind for 15 minutes, then remove the paper and baking beans and bake for a further 5–10 minutes until set and golden. Remove the pastry case from the oven and egg wash the hot pastry base. Set aside to cool.

Skin the peaches and cut in half, removing the stones. Cut each half into four wedges. Put the peaches into a frying pan with the sugar. Set over a low heat and gently cook until the sugar has dissolved and the peaches softened. Allow to cool.

Continued overleaf

To make the coulis, combine the raspberries, icing sugar and lemon juice in a saucepan. Cook over a medium heat for about 5 minutes, stirring occasionally, until the icing sugar has dissolved and the raspberries softened. Mash the raspberries down. Leave lumpy (I prefer a lumpy coulis) or press through a sieve to remove the seeds. Set aside.

Now make the Italian meringue. Use the lemon half to thoroughly wipe down the large mixing bowl and whisk attachment of a free-standing electric mixer. Put the 4 egg whites in the bowl and turn on the mixer to whisk the whites to soft, fluffy peaks.

While the whites are being whisked, heat the sugar and 5 tablespoons of water in a saucepan. Once the sugar has dissolved, bring to a rolling boil and boil the syrup until the temperature reaches 118°C (244°F). Remove from the heat. With the mixer on a medium/high speed, slowly and carefully pour the boiling hot sugar syrup down the side of the mixing bowl into the whisked egg whites. When all the hot sugar syrup has been added, continue to whisk until the meringue mixture has cooled and is thick – it should make stiff and glossy peaks that keep their shape when the bowl is turned upside down.

Spoon the peach filling over the bottom of the pastry case and top with the fresh raspberries (reserve a few raspberries for the decoration). Either spoon on the Italian meringue in soft peaks or pipe it on in your chosen design, making sure the middle peaks are higher. Use a kitchen blowtorch to give the meringue a golden finish and crisp up the peaks. Sprinkle with the lemon zest and top with the reserved raspberries.

Serve immediately with a drizzle of raspberry coulis.

Gooseberry fool éclairs

The humble gooseberry is often overlooked or just whacked into a crumble. Lovely as a crumble is, I thought I would make gooseberries the star of the show in a delicate éclair. You can use physalis (also known as Cape gooseberries), if you prefer: they are usually just used for decoration but offer so much more than that, being sweet yet tangy and a beautiful amber colour.

Makes 20

—

Choux:
55g unsalted butter
1 tsp vanilla bean paste
75g plain flour
pinch of salt
2 eggs

Filling/topping:
200g gooseberries or
    Cape gooseberries
    (physalis), cut in half
finely grated zest and
    juice of 1 lemon
1 tbsp caster sugar
200ml double cream
200g white chocolate,
    broken into pieces
50g fresh blackberries

Preheat the oven to 190°C fan (210°C/420°F/Gas Mark 6/7). Line two baking sheets with greaseproof paper.

Put the butter, vanilla and 160ml water in a large saucepan over a medium heat and allow the butter to melt, then bring to the boil. Meanwhile, sift the flour and salt on to a folded piece of greaseproof paper.

When the buttery water is at boiling point, remove from the heat and in one go tip the flour into the pan. Mix vigorously with a wooden spoon until the mixture leaves the sides of the pan and forms a soft ball. Return to a low heat and continue to stir the balled mixture for about 1 minute.

Transfer the hot mix to a bowl and stir a little to help it cool down. When the mixture has cooled slightly, beat in one egg using a handheld electric mixer until the egg is incorporated and the mixture starts to look thick and glossy. (It may look like it is curdling but keep beating and it will come together.) Add the second egg and beat again until the choux dough is smooth, thick and glossy. It should drop off a spoon slowly and hold its shape.

Spoon the dough into a piping bag and snip a 2cm opening in the end. Pipe out 10–15cm strips on the lined baking sheets, leaving a little space between each one.

Bake for 25–30 minutes until golden, risen and crisp. Transfer to a wire rack to cool.

Put the gooseberries or Cape gooseberries in a small saucepan with the lemon juice and sugar. Cook over a low heat until the fruit has softened and the mix has reduced. Remove from the heat and allow to cool.

Whip up the double cream with the lemon zest until thick.

Melt the white chocolate in a heatproof bowl set over a small saucepan of boiling water. Remove from the heat.

Split the éclairs open down the middle. Spoon the cream into a piping bag. Pipe a line of cream in the bottom half of each éclair. Spoon a little of the gooseberry mixture on top of the cream. Dip the top of the other half of the éclair in the chocolate, then set it on top of the cream and gooseberry mixture. Alternatively, set the top of the éclair in place and drizzle a zigzag of chocolate over it. Push a blackberry into the centre of each éclair to finish.

*Gooseberries are mainly available June—July. However, Cape gooseberries (physalis) can be found all year round and they make a great alternative. But swap the fruit for whatever you like or what is in season.

When I eat out, I look at the pudding menu before I look at the main menu. I've always done this. I want to make sure I have room for pudding, especially if there is a new one I want to try. More often than not I'll have pudding whether I have room or not. I have even been known to order several and pretend they are for other people! So making puddings at home is pure joy for me. I particularly like to be able to bake puddings that have a double use – served warm with a heap of ice cream or hot custard as a pudding and then cold as an afternoon treat.

—

Some of my preserves go hand in hand with my puddings, like the mango curd used in my **Mango and Raspberry Pavlova** (page 127) or the jam in my **Cherry Amaretto Bakewell Tart** (page 93). Home-made preserves are so easy to make and a great thing to have in the fridge as they can be used in many a bake. My **Vanilla Custard** features in this chapter too – it really is the most perfect accompaniment to most of my puddings and a key ingredient in a few of my bakes too.

Puddings & preserves

Toffee apple crumble

This is one toffee apple recipe that won't break your teeth. Softened tangy apples and a smooth, creamy toffee sauce under a traditional crunchy crumble with added dates that trick you into thinking they are pieces of chewy toffee! Serve hot with custard and a double helping of toffee sauce, then go back for seconds! You can also use pears if you like. They may not need softening if they are very ripe.

Serves 8

Toffee:
60g light soft brown sugar
60g dark soft brown sugar
120g unsalted butter
100ml double cream

Apples:
4 Bramley apples, peeled, cored and cut into chunks
4 eating apples, peeled, cored and cut into chunks
knob of unsalted butter
1 tsp ground cinnamon

Crumble:
250g plain flour
200g unsalted butter, softened
100g golden caster sugar
50g demerara sugar
50g stoneless dates, chopped
50g rolled oats
50g pecan nuts, chopped

Preheat the oven to 160°C fan (180°C/350°F/Gas Mark 4).

First make the toffee. Put both types of sugar and the butter in a saucepan and melt over a low heat until the sugar has dissolved. Turn the heat up to medium. When the mixture is frothy and bubbling, remove from the heat and stir in the double cream. Allow to cool.

Tip the apples into a large saucepan and add the knob of butter and cinnamon plus 1 tablespoon of water if the pan looks a bit dry. Allow to soften over a low heat for 10 minutes, stirring occasionally.

For the crumble, sift the flour into a large bowl, add the butter and rub in with your fingertips until the mixture resembles breadcrumbs. Add both types of sugars, the dates and oats and mix, scrunching everything together to make lumps of crumble.

Transfer the apple mix to an ovenproof dish (about 25–30cm) and drizzle over half of the toffee. Spread the crumble mix evenly on top but don't press down – it should be lumpy and bumpy. Scatter over the chopped pecans. Bake for 25–30 minutes until the fruit is bubbling around the edge and the crumble is golden brown.

Serve hot with Vanilla Custard (opposite) and the rest of the toffee.

Vanilla custard

School dinner puddings drenched in custard were always my favourite, and cold custard out of a tin was always a really naughty treat for me. I still love it but I'd now rather have this most vanilla-y, creamy custard that I make myself. It can be served as an accompaniment to crumbles and pies or to make my Raspberry and Custard Almond Cake (page 50) or Apple and Pear Crumble Muffins (page 61).

Makes about 450ml
—

300ml whole milk
300ml double cream
1 tsp vanilla bean paste
30g golden caster sugar
3 egg yolks
2 tsp cornflour

Stir together the milk, cream and vanilla in a heavy-based medium-sized saucepan. Set over a low/medium heat and stir until just boiling.

In a bowl mix together the sugar, egg yolks and cornflour to make a smooth paste.

Pour a small amount of the hot milk and cream mix into the yolk mix and stir through. Add a little more and mix, then pour in the rest of the hot milk, stirring to incorporate it. If you have any lumps you can strain the mixture.

Rinse and dry the saucepan, then pour the mixture back in. Set over a low heat and stir until the custard is thick and smooth.

Plum, nectarine & ginger crumble

A cross between a cobbler and a crumble, this fruity little hybrid is a family favourite, and I often swap the fruits around to include those in season. It's even better the next day when the nectarines really take on the flavour of the ginger. The balance ensures that you get a fruit-infused layer of stodge just where the crumble meets the fruit and then the crunchy crumble and granola on top. I drown mine in custard but you can serve it with cream, ice cream or even a scoop of crème fraîche.

Serves 8

6 plums
4 nectarines
20g crystallised stem
  ginger, cut into small
  pieces
1 star anise
1 cinnamon stick,
  broken in half
2 tbsp runny honey
150g plain flour
50g rolled oats
100g light soft brown
  sugar
1 tsp ground ginger
50g unsalted butter,
  melted
1 egg
50g Granola (page 84)

Preheat the oven to 160°C fan (180°C/350°F/Gas Mark 4).

Cut the plums into quarters, removing the stones. Cut each nectarine into eight wedges, removing the stones.

Mix together the plums, nectarines and crystallised ginger in an ovenproof dish. Add the star anise and broken cinnamon stick, and drizzle over some runny honey. Cover with foil and bake for 20–30 minutes to start softening the fruit.

*If the fruit is lovely and ripe, you may not need to pre-cook it to soften it. Simply cover the uncooked fruit with the crumble mix and bake for 30–35 minutes.

Meanwhile, combine the flour, oats, sugar and ground ginger in a mixing bowl. Add the melted butter and mix together. Add the egg, then get your hands in and scrunch it all together. Add the granola and work this through until you have a moist crumble.

Remove the fruit from the oven. Tip the crumble mix over the top and even it out, leaving lots of lumps and bumps. Return to the oven and bake for 30–35 minutes until the fruit is bubbling and the crumble is golden brown on top.

Serve with my home-made Vanilla Custard (page 121) – or for a little change make it a cinnamon custard by swapping the vanilla for 1 teaspoon ground cinnamon.

Marmalade, cardamom & chocolate bread & butter pudding

Rich and chocolatey with just a little bit of spice. There's nothing wrong with the original bread and butter pudding with sultanas, but once you have tried this version with orange marmalade, chocolate and cardamom you may never go back.

Serves 6–8

—

300ml whole milk
300ml double cream
1 tsp vanilla bean paste
6 cardamom pods, bashed
2 whole eggs
2 egg yolks
2 tbsp golden caster sugar
1 small loaf crusty white bread
softened unsalted butter
good-quality fine-cut marmalade
70g dark chocolate chips
1 tbsp demerara sugar
grated zest of 1 orange

Put the milk, cream, vanilla and bashed cardamom pods in a medium-sized saucepan. Slowly bring to the boil over a low heat, then simmer for a couple of minutes. Remove from the heat and leave to infuse and cool for about 10 minutes.

Meanwhile, beat together the eggs, egg yolks and caster sugar in a large mixing bowl.

Strain some of the creamy milk mixture into the egg and sugar mix, then whisk together. Strain in the rest of the creamy milk and whisk gently to mix the custard. Set aside.

Cut the loaf into about eight slices and butter each slice. Spread marmalade over each slice – as little or as much as you like. Cut each slice in half diagonally so you have two triangles.

Grease an ovenproof dish with unsalted butter. Layer the bread triangles in the dish so they slightly overlap each other and fit snugly together. Sprinkle the chocolate chips over the bread, making sure some get in between the slices. Pour the warm custard evenly over the top, then leave to soak for 30 minutes.

Preheat the oven to 160°C fan (180°C/350°F/Gas Mark 4).

Bash together the demerara sugar and orange zest in a pestle and mortar. Sprinkle over the bread and butter pudding. Bake for 25–30 minutes until the edges are golden and crisp and the custard has thickened.

Enjoy hot with extra custard (see Vanilla Custard, page 121), scoops of vanilla ice cream or some pouring cream.

Sticky toffee pudding

This is my number-one choice on a pudding menu. Even if I am full to the brim I will always order it with a big scoop of vanilla ice cream and eat every last bit. This great version has super-soft sponge and is self-saucing so when you flip it over you get the gorgeous shiny sauce on top, just wait a moment before tucking in or you'll burn your tongue!

Serves 8

—

Sauce:
120g unsalted butter
120g dark soft brown sugar
120ml double cream
45g pecan nuts

Sponge:
250g stoneless dates
  (50g of them chopped)
200ml boiling water
1 tsp bicarbonate soda
75g unsalted butter,
  softened
150g light soft brown
  sugar
1 tbsp golden syrup
2 eggs
200g plain flour
1 tsp baking powder
¼ tsp ground cinnamon
¼ tsp freshly grated
  nutmeg
30g pecan nuts, chopped

Preheat the oven to 160°C fan (180°C/350°F/Gas Mark 4).

First make the sauce. Put the butter and sugar in a saucepan and cook over a medium heat until the butter has melted and sugar dissolved. Keep bubbling away until the mixture starts to look frothy. Remove from the heat and whisk in the double cream until smooth.

Pour the sauce into a 25cm square ovenproof dish. Arrange the whole pecans in the sauce in lines. Place in the freezer to set.

Put the 200g whole stoned dates in a bowl, pour over the boiling water and add the bicarbonate of soda. Leave to soak for 5–10 minutes until softened, then blitz the mixture in a food processor or blender until smooth.

Combine the butter, sugar and golden syrup in a large bowl and beat together until light and fluffy. Add the eggs one at a time, beating well, followed by the puréed dates. Mix through the flour, baking powder, cinnamon and nutmeg. Finally, fold through the chopped dates and pecans.

Remove the dish with the now-set sauce from the freezer. Turn the sponge mix into the dish and spread evenly. Bake for 25–35 minutes until a skewer inserted into the middle comes out clean (do not poke all the way through as there is a sauce layer at the bottom).

Allow to cool slightly, then turn the whole thing out on to a plate so the sauce and whole pecans are now on top and drizzling down the sides. Serve warm with vanilla ice cream or my Vanilla Custard (page 121).

Mango & raspberry Pavlova

Pavlova – or any meringues for that matter – is my Mam and my sister's favourite. It reminds me of Christmas when they would argue over who got the last meringue nest filled with raspberries and cream. I prefer a meringue with a softer centre but if you like a crunchy meringue simply bake it a little longer.

Serves a lot!

—

Meringue:
* 400g white caster sugar
200g golden caster sugar
½ lemon, to wipe bowl and whisk
10 egg whites, at room temperature
1 tsp cream of tartar
2 tsp cornflour
50g freeze-dried raspberries

* *Darker sugar gives a darker meringue with a more caramel flavour, but it will be softer!*

Preheat the oven to 160°C fan (180°C/350°F/Gas Mark 4). Spread out both types of caster sugar on a large baking tray and heat in the oven for about 10 minutes until the sugar starts to melt around the edges.

Meanwhile, use the lemon half to rub the inside of the bowl of a free-standing electric mixer fitted with a whisk attachment. Wipe the whisk with lemon too. This will remove any grease. Put the egg whites into the bowl and whisk on a medium speed until fluffy and cloud-like.

Remove the hot sugar from the oven and reduce the temperature to 120°C fan (140°C/275°F/Gas Mark 1). Slowly add the hot sugar to the egg whites, a spoonful at a time, whisking all the while. Once all the sugar has been incorporated, continue whisking until the meringue is stiff and glossy.

Add the cream of tartar and cornflour and mix in. If you rub a bit of meringue between your fingers it should be smooth and not grainy. Check for stiffness by lifting out the whisk – the meringue on it should hold high pointy peaks (or, if you are feeling brave, lift the bowl up and turn it upside down – the meringue should not fall out).

You now need two large non-stick silicone baking sheets (or baking sheets lined with baking parchment). Spoon two-thirds of the meringue on to one silicone sheet and spread to make a large disc about 30cm in diameter with a dip in the centre and slightly higher edges.

Fold the freeze-dried raspberries into the remaining meringue and spoon it into a piping bag fitted with a large round nozzle. Pipe in a

Continued overleaf

Continued...

Filling:
400ml double cream
200g mascarpone cheese
20g icing sugar
400g fresh raspberries
about 200g Mango Curd
   (page 154)
4 passion fruit
fresh mint sprigs

smaller disc, about 20cm in diameter, on the second silicone sheet, drawing up the meringue to get lovely high points around the edge.

Place in the oven and straightaway reduce the temperature to 100°C fan (120°C/250°F/Gas Mark ½). Dry out for 2½–3 hours, depending on how soft or crunchy you like your meringue. Turn off the oven and leave the meringues inside until they are completely cooled (overnight if possible).

For the filling, whip the double cream in a large bowl until stiff and smooth. Fold in the mascarpone and icing sugar. Add 300g of the raspberries and fold these through, bashing some up as you go.

Place the larger meringue disc on a serving plate and pile two-thirds of the raspberry-laden cream filling on it, in the dipped centre. Dot half of the mango curd on top of the filling and swirl through using a sharp knife. Drips and dribbles are good. Gently set the smaller meringue disc on top and spoon on the remaining cream and raspberry filling. Swirl through the rest of the mango curd.

Decorate with the remaining whole raspberries, adding them to both top and bottom. Scoop out the passion fruit flesh and drizzle over the lumps and bumps of cream and raspberries. Add a couple of mint sprigs and dig in straight away!

You don't have to heat the sugar up before adding it to the egg whites but I find it helps to stabilise it and gives a good head start!

Red, white & blue meringues

Unlike the giant Pavlova these are the perfect size to pop straight in your mouth in one go and generally this is what tends to happen! You can vary the size and shape with the help of some creative piping nozzles, to create toppings for cakes, cupcakes or just more sweet treats! The meringues are great to package up as gifts but not with cream or jam/curd in the middle as this will make them go soft quite quickly.

Makes 24—30, or 12—15 sandwiched meringues

—

115g caster sugar
½ lemon, to wipe bowl and whisk
3 egg whites
45g icing sugar
red and blue food colouring gel
300ml double cream
blueberry jam, preferably home-made (see my Jam Jam Jam page 152)
Mango Curd (page 154) or ready-made passion fruit curd
sprinkles (e.g. finely chopped nuts, hundreds and thousands, mini chocolate stars)

Preheat the oven to 160°C fan (180°C/350°F/Gas Mark 4).

Spread out the caster sugar on a baking tray and heat in the oven for about 10 minutes until the sugar starts to melt around the edges.

Meanwhile, use the lemon half to rub the inside of the bowl of a free-standing electric mixer fitted with a whisk attachment. Wipe the whisk with lemon too. This will remove any grease. Put the egg whites into the bowl and whisk on a medium speed until fluffy with firm peaks.

Remove the hot sugar from the oven and reduce the temperature to 100°C fan (120°C/250°F/Gas Mark ½). Slowly add the hot sugar to the egg whites, a spoonful at a time, whisking all the while on a medium speed. Once all the sugar has been incorporated, continue whisking until the meringue is stiff and glossy. Add the icing sugar a spoonful at a time while whisking.

Check for stiffness by lifting out the whisk – the meringue on it should hold high pointy peaks (or, if you are feeling brave, lift the bowl up and turn it upside down – the meringue should not fall out).

Fit three piping bags with nozzles of your choice – I like to use a large round one or a flower nozzle. Paint a stripe of blue food colouring gel on the inside of one piping bag and a stripe of red gel inside the second bag (or use colours of your choice); leave the third bag bare. Divide the meringue equally between the piping bags.

* Create your own colours on a small plate before brushing into the piping bag. The gel colours are very concentrated so you need only a very small amount — otherwise the meringues may be quite psychedelic!!! ⌣

Line two baking sheets with greaseproof paper – stick the paper in place with a smudge of meringue. Pipe out small rounds or flowers in red, white and blue. Feel free to make different shapes for each colour. You'll need an even number of meringues.

Dry out the meringues in the oven for about 2 hours until crisp on the outside. Then turn the oven off and leave the meringues inside to cool – you can speed this up by propping open the oven door with a wooden spoon.

Once the meringues are cool, whip the double cream until stiff and smooth. Spoon into a piping bag fitted with a nozzle of your choice. Pipe some cream on the base of a meringue and add a little jam or curd, then press the base of another meringue on to this. Sprinkle what you like around the edge so it sticks to the cream, or leave the meringues plain.

If you're not filling with jam/curd and cream, you can dip the base of each meringue in melted chocolate.

Photo overleaf →

Individual banoffee pies

Here's a complete and utter family favourite! My Mam always used to make banoffee pie – she'd make the caramel by boiling a can of condensed milk... until one time when she let it boil dry and it exploded! So I now make the banoffee pie in our family!! This recipe makes individual pies, although you can make one big one if you prefer.

Makes 8

—

Filo (if you are feeling brave!):
300g strong white
    bread flour
½ tsp salt
1½ tbsp light olive oil
150–180ml warm water
100g cornflour
100g unsalted butter,
    melted, to assemble

Or: a 270g pack of ready-
    made filo pastry sheets,
    thawed if frozen

Salted caramel:
120g unsalted butter
120g dark soft brown sugar
50g dark chocolate
    (minimum 70% cocoa
    solids), chopped
100ml double cream
pinch of rock salt

Filling:
300ml double cream
½ tsp vanilla bean paste
4 ripe bananas
toasted flaked almonds
grated dark chocolate
    (minimum 70% cocoa
    solids)

If you are making your own filo, sift the flour and salt into the bowl of a free-standing electric mixer fitted with a dough hook and make a well in the centre. Mix together the oil and warm water. Turn the mixer on to slow speed and slowly pour in the water/oil mix. Continue mixing on slow speed to bring the ingredients together, then turn up to medium speed and mix/knead for 6–7 minutes until the dough is smooth and stretchy. While you are mixing, add either more warm water or more flour if the dough is too wet or too dry to come together. Wrap the dough in cling film and leave to rest in a cool place for at least 30 minutes.

For the caramel, melt the butter with the brown sugar in a large saucepan over a medium heat, swirling the mixture in the pan to prevent sticking. When the sugar has dissolved, allow the mixture to bubble and froth until it turns to a golden caramel colour. Add the dark chocolate and remove from the heat, then pour in the double cream and whisk thoroughly. Add the salt and stir through. Transfer to a bowl, then place in the fridge to cool and thicken.

Now return to the filo. Divide the dough into 8–10 pieces. (Keep the pieces covered with cling film to prevent them from drying out.) Turn a pasta machine to its widest setting, then feed one piece of filo dough through. Repeat the rolling, each time turning down the setting by a notch. After four or five times through the rollers, lay the pastry sheet flat and dust with cornflour before continuing with the rolling. When the sheet of filo is the perfect thinness (0.5mm/setting 9), lay it on a baking sheet. Immediately cover with a slightly dampened tea towel or cling film to prevent it from drying out.

Continued overleaf

Repeat the rolling with a second piece of pastry. Dust the first filo sheet with cornflour, then lay the second sheet on top. Cover this with the damp tea towel or cling film. Continue in this way until you've used all the pastry, dusting with cornflour between each layer and always covering with the tea towel or cling film.

If using shop-bought filo, unwrap and separate the sheets, then cover with a damp tea towel. Leave to warm up to room temperature.

Preheat the oven to 160°C fan (180°C/350°F/Gas Mark 4). Lightly grease a 12-hole muffin tin.

Cut each sheet of handmade or shop-bought filo into 10 x 10cm squares (four or five squares per hole of the muffin tin is perfect, which means you need to cut 48–60 squares in total). Push a square into each hole of the muffin tin to line the bottom and sides. Brush the filo with melted butter, then place a second square of filo on top but at a slightly different angle so all the corners are sticking up. Brush this filo square with melted butter. Continue adding filo squares, each at a different angle and slightly scrunching the edges, and brushing with butter until you have four or five layers of filo in each hole of the muffin tin.

Bake for 8–10 minutes until the pastry is golden. Remove from the oven and allow to cool.

To make the filling, whip the double cream with the vanilla bean paste until smooth and thick. Spoon into a piping bag fitted with a round nozzle. Slice the bananas.

Place a teaspoon of caramel into the bottom of each pastry case. Add slices of banana, then pipe on vanilla cream in a little swirl. Sprinkle with toasted flaked almonds and finish with grated dark chocolate. Serve immediately.

Bramble apple pie

A traditional pie, nothing more and nothing less! I like to use brambles, which are sweet-sharp wild blackberries – we often pick these when out on a walk, and I freeze some to have in reserve. You can of course use fresh blackberries. If you are like my Dad then you'll want this with lashings of cream. Hot custard (see recipe on page 121) is my favourite.

Serves 6–8

—

Shortcrust pastry:
300g plain flour, plus extra for dusting
pinch of salt
150g cold unsalted butter, cut into cubes
30g golden caster sugar
finely grated zest and juice of 1 lemon
2 egg yolks
beaten egg, for egg wash

Filling:
4 Bramley apples
knob of unsalted butter
1 tbsp light soft brown sugar
1 star anise
250g brambles or blackberries
demerara sugar, for sprinkling

To make the pastry, put the flour and salt into a large bowl, add the butter and rub in with your fingertips until the mixture looks like breadcrumbs. Add the caster sugar and lemon zest and mix in with a table knife, then add the egg yolks and mix together with the knife. If the dough isn't quite coming together, add cold water a teaspoon at a time.

Now get your hands in and bring the dough together, but try not to knead it too much. Shape into a thick disc, wrap in cling film and chill for about an hour.

Peel and core the apples, then cut each into eight wedges. Put these in a pan with the butter, brown sugar, lemon juice and star anise. Cook over a low heat for 15–20 minutes until the sugar has dissolved and the apples have started to soften. Remove from the heat and stir through the brambles, then allow to cool fully.

Preheat the oven to 180°C fan (200°C/400°F/Gas Mark 6).

Cut the pastry into two portions, one a bit larger than the other. Flour the work surface and roll out the larger piece to about 3mm thick. Use the rolling pin to lift the pastry up and drape it into a 15 x 15cm pie tin with a rim. Gently press the pastry into the tin to line it. Trim off any excess pastry. Roll out the other piece of pastry and cut out a lid for the pie – it should be a bit bigger than the tin.

Tip the now cooled apple and bramble filling into the pastry case (remove the star anise). Egg wash the edge of the case. Gently lift the pie lid with the help of the rolling pin and lay it over the filling. Crimp the edges together using a fork and trim off any excess pastry (you can cut some leaf and apple shapes from the trimmings and stick these to the pastry lid with a little egg wash).

Egg wash the pastry lid and sprinkle with the demerara sugar. Using a sharp knife, poke two small holes in the centre of the lid to allow steam to escape during baking. Place in the oven and bake for 50–60 minutes until the pastry is golden brown. If the pastry starts to brown too much, cover with foil. Serve hot.

Hidden clove, apple & strawberry strudel

My Dad hates cloves, and whenever Nan made apple strudel he would always ask if there were any cloves in it. Nan always said no. But lo and behold, with his first bite my Dad would always get the clove! Nan would laugh as she said 'Oh, I don't know how that got in there!' and wink at me. That solitary clove adds a subtle, spicy fragrance.

Serves 8

—

150g plain flour, plus extra
   for dusting
150g strong white bread
   flour
1 tsp icing sugar
50g lard, cubed
150ml cold water
200g cold unsalted butter

Filling:
2 Bramley apples
2 Braeburn apples
100g fresh strawberries
grated zest and juice of
   1 lemon
1 clove
40g golden caster sugar
½ tsp ground cinnamon
40g ground almonds
50g unsalted butter

To finish:
1 egg, beaten with a splash
   of milk, for egg wash
25g demerara sugar
25g flaked almonds

First make the pastry. Sift both types of flour and the icing sugar into a large bowl. Add the lard and rub in with your fingertips until the mixture resembles breadcrumbs. Stir in the cold water and bring everything together with your hands. Turn out the dough on to a lightly floured work surface and knead briefly until smooth. Wrap in cling film and chill for 30 minutes.

Meanwhile, place the cold butter between two pieces of greaseproof paper and bash/roll with a rolling pin until you have a flat 15 x 25cm rectangle that is about 3mm thick.

Roll out the chilled dough on the floured surface (rolling away from you) to a 20 x 40cm rectangle. Lay the butter rectangle on the bottom two-thirds of the dough rectangle. There should be a clear border of about 1cm at the bottom and 2.5cm at the sides.

Fold the top, unbuttered third of the dough rectangle down over the middle third, then fold the bottom third up over the middle third (you will now have alternating layers of dough, butter, dough, butter, dough). Pinch the edges together, then wrap and chill for 30 minutes.

Flour the work surface again and set the dough on it so a short side is nearest to you. Roll out away from you into a 20 x 40cm rectangle again. This time fold both the top and bottom of the rectangle in so they meet in the middle, then fold in half like a book. Pinch the edges together. Wrap and chill for 30 minutes.

Continued overleaf

Continued...

Roll out the dough into a rectangle as before. Fold the top third down and the bottom third up over it. Wrap and chill for 30 minutes. Repeat this rolling and folding process (called a 'turn') three times, chilling in between for 30 minutes. This will make a total of four turns.

You only need about two-thirds of the pastry for this recipe, so cut it into two pieces: one third and two thirds. Keep the larger piece you are going to use for the strudel in the fridge until you need it. The other piece can be frozen – you could use it to make Stilton Twisted Straws (page 158) or to top a Choose-your-lid Chicken Pie (see recipe on page 196).

Preheat the oven to 180°C fan (200°C/400°F/Gas Mark 6). Line a baking sheet with greaseproof paper.

Peel, core and dice the apples. Hull and quarter the strawberries. Put the fruit in a large bowl with the lemon zest and juice, clove, caster sugar and cinnamon. Mix together gently.

Lightly dust a work surface and roll out the pastry away from you into a 30 x 20cm rectangle that is about 3mm thick. Lightly mark a line down the centre of the rectangle to divide it in half lengthways. Sprinkle the ground almonds evenly over one half, leaving about a 1cm clear border around the edges. Spoon the apple and strawberry mixture, slightly heaped up, in a line on top of the ground almonds. Dot small pieces of butter over the fruit.

Egg wash all of the pastry edges, then fold the empty side up and over the filled side. Press the edges together using a fork to crimp. Carefully transfer to the baking sheet. Egg wash the whole strudel. Using a very sharp knife, make cuts across the top of the strudel at 2.5cm intervals. Sprinkle the demerara sugar and flaked almonds over the top.

Bake for 35–40 minutes until the pastry has puffed up and is golden and crisp.

Serve hot with my Vanilla Custard (page 121) and wait to see who gets the hidden clove!

The 3 P's roulade

My tangy passion fruit curd plays a starring roll (get it?) in this summery roulade. Pomegranate seeds that look like little gems pop in your mouth to contrast with the smooth curd. If you do get a crack while rolling, don't worry – the melted white chocolate drizzle and pistachios will hide it.

Serves 8

—

4 large eggs
120g golden caster sugar, plus extra for dusting
120g self-raising flour, sifted
finely grated zest of 1 lemon
50g shelled pistachios
300ml double cream
25g icing sugar, sifted
1/2 tsp vanilla bean paste
4 tbsp Passion Fruit Curd (page 155)
seeds of 1 pomegranate
50g white chocolate, broken into pieces

*Don't skip the sugar-dusting stage before you flip the sponge out or it will stick to the greaseproof paper when it comes to unrolling and filling.

Preheat the oven to 170°C fan (190°C/375°F/Gas Mark 5). Grease a 30 x 24cm Swiss roll tin and line with baking parchment.

Put the eggs and caster sugar in a mixing bowl and, using an electric mixer, beat for 5–6 minutes until doubled in volume and the mixture is at ribbon stage – when you lift the whisk out, the mixture should fall back in ribbons that sit on top of the mix in the bowl.

Using a large metal spoon, fold in the flour in three batches, making sure it is all incorporated. Add the lemon zest with the last addition of flour.

Gently pour the mixture into the prepared tin and spread evenly using a spatula. Bake for 12–15 minutes until just firm and light golden brown.

Line a large baking sheet with greaseproof paper and dust it with caster sugar. Gently turn the sponge out on to the sugared paper. Carefully peel away the baking parchment used to line the tin. Leave the oven on.

Use a blunt knife to gently press a line in the sponge parallel to one short end and about 2.5cm away from it. Fold the edge of the sugared paper over the sponge at that end, then roll up the cake with the paper inside. Allow the rolled cake to cool completely.

Spread the pistachio nuts on a small baking tray and toast in the oven for about 10 minutes. Leave to cool, then roughly chop.

Combine the cream, sifted icing sugar and vanilla bean paste in a large bowl and whip until stiff and light.

Gently unroll the now cooled sponge. Spread the cream evenly over the sponge, leaving about 2.5cm clear at the short side with the marked line. Dot the passion fruit curd over the cream and swirl in using a blunt knife. Scatter the pomegranate seeds over the cream and curd.

Starting at the short side with the marked line, gently roll over and tuck under the first 2.5cm of cake, then tightly roll up the sponge (try not to squash out too much filling). If it cracks do not worry – it adds character!

Melt the white chocolate in a heatproof bowl set over a saucepan of simmering water. Drizzle it all over the roulade. While the chocolate is still wet, sprinkle the pistachios all over. If you have leftover pomegranate seeds, add these too. Serve immediately.

Photo overleaf →

Lime & kiwi cheesecake

I hate cheesecake. There, I said it! So why have I included this in my book?, you ask. Well, I love baking for everyone else and everyone else seems to love cheesecake. I wanted to keep it as simple and fresh as possible so I added lime to cut through the cheese mix and fresh and tangy kiwi. Rather than crush up shop-bought biscuits I've made my own. They're so much better and really take this 'yummy' cheesecake up a notch (yummy for everyone else).

Serves 10–12

Base:
150g plain flour
75g ground almonds
185g cold unsalted butter, cut into cubes
100g golden caster sugar
½ tsp ground cinnamon
2 tsp cold water

Filling:
500g full-fat soft cheese
100g icing sugar, sifted
finely grated zest and juice of 3 limes
300ml double cream
6 kiwi fruits
shreds of lime zest to finish

Preheat the oven to 170°C fan (190°C/375°F/Gas Mark 5).

For the base, mix together the flour and ground almonds in a bowl. Add the cubed butter and rub in with your fingertips until you have a breadcrumb consistency. Stir through the sugar and cinnamon. Add the water and mix in with a fork – the mixture should resemble damp sand.

Tip on to a baking sheet and spread out, but don't press down. Bake for 20–25 minutes until golden brown. Stir around a couple of times during baking so the mix maintains its sand-like, loose texture. Tip the still-hot mix into a 30cm round or square, loose-bottomed flan tin and gently press down to make an even layer on the bottom. Leave to cool and set.

To make the filling, combine the soft cheese, sifted icing sugar, lime zest and juice in a bowl. Whisk together until smooth. In a separate bowl whip the double cream until thick. Fold the cream gently into the soft cheese mix until evenly combined.

Tip the filling mix on top of the cooled base in the tin and smooth out evenly. Chill for at least 6 hours, preferably overnight, until set.

Peel the kiwi fruits and slice either into rounds or stars. Layer these on top of the set cheesecake filling. Sprinkle over some lime zest to finish.

Chocolate & banana waffles

The sweet to my savoury! This is the waffle version of the much-loved chocolate and banana pancake! It's a combination that works so well, and folding the banana through the batter gives a lovely rich flavour. The addition of granola is a nice breakfast crunch.

Makes 5—10
(depending on the size
of your waffle-maker)
—

250g plain flour
1 tsp baking powder
1 tbsp golden caster sugar
pinch of salt
1 tsp ground cinnamon
2 eggs
40g unsalted butter
450ml whole milk
3 bananas, 1 lightly
   mashed and 2 sliced
oil, for greasing
chocolate-hazelnut
   spread
handful of Granola
   (page 84)

Sift the flour, baking powder, sugar, salt and cinnamon into a large bowl. Make a well in the centre. Crack the eggs into the well.

Melt the butter, then add to the milk. Pour into the well. Whisk together to make a smooth batter. Set aside for 30 minutes.

Heat your waffle-maker according to the manufacturer's directions.

Fold the lightly mashed banana through the batter. Brush the waffle-maker with a little oil to prevent sticking (unless it is non-stick), then add some of the batter. Dot with a little chocolate-hazelnut spread (or drizzle it if it is runny enough), then cover with more batter. Close the waffle-maker and cook for 3—4 minutes until the waffle is golden brown (turn the waffle-maker on to its other side halfway through if it is a stove-top type).

Remove the waffle, top with sliced banana and more chocolate-hazelnut spread, and sprinkle with granola. Serve straight away.

Ivy's Malteser ice cream

This is to honour my Nan, Ivy, who we sadly lost at the age of 93. Her diet mainly consisted of sugar, chocolate mousse and Maltesers and she led a happy, long life just like that. So this recipe is for her. If you can't get hold of Maltesers Malty Hot Chocolate you can use regular hot chocolate but the actual Maltesers are essential, and do not hold back on the amount. Nan wouldn't eat anything else and would definitely know the difference! Smooth and rich with that lovely crunch of honeycomb that she so very much loved.

Serves 6

—

300ml double cream
300ml whole milk
5 egg yolks (you can use the egg whites for meringues)
50g Maltesers Malty Hot Chocolate powder (2 x 25g sachets)
1 tsp vanilla bean paste
100g Maltesers, crushed
1 tbsp salted caramel (see Individual Banoffee Pies, page 135, or Millionaire Shortbread Hearts, page 83), or bought ready-made caramel sauce

*If you do not have an ice-cream maker you can pour the cooled custard into a freezer-proof container and freeze. You will need to stir the ice cream every 30—40 minutes during the freezing process to ensure it doesn't crystallise.

Depending on the type of ice-cream maker you have, you may need to put the base in the freezer at least 24 hours prior to starting.

Pour the cream and milk into a small saucepan and set over a medium heat. Warm until just boiling.

Meanwhile, whisk together the egg yolks, chocolate powder and vanilla in a mixing bowl. Once the creamy milk starts to boil, slowly pour it in a steady stream over the yolk mix, whisking the whole time.

Pour the mix back into the saucepan and set over a low heat. Whisk constantly until you have a thickened custard. Allow to cool.

Slowly pour the cooled custard into the ice-cream maker and churn for 20 minutes. Add the crushed chocolates and churn for a further 5 minutes. The ice cream should now be thickened and semi-frozen.

Pour the ice cream into a freezer-proof container. Drizzle over the caramel and swirl through quickly with a knife. Place in the freezer and leave to firm up (or you can eat it soft straight away, if you prefer).

Serve with warm cookies, such as my Chewy Chocolate Orange Cookies (page 77), or alongside a wedge of my Date and Ginger Cake (page 37).

Red grapefruit & elderflower sorbet

I have a slight obsession with sorbet, and can eat a whole tub in one sitting. The sharpness of the red grapefruit in this sorbet works in perfect balance with the soft and subtle flavour of the elderflower liqueur. I come across elderflower liqueur at a food festival and Chase do some lovely variations. Try adding a dash to a glass of champagne too.

Serves 6
—

250g golden caster sugar
finely grated zest and juice
  of 1 lemon
juice of 2 red grapefruits
100ml elderflower liqueur
1 egg white

Depending on the type of ice-cream maker you have, you may need to put the base in the freezer at least 24 hours prior to starting.

Combine the sugar, lemon zest and 450ml water in a saucepan. Set on a medium heat and allow the sugar to dissolve, then bring to the boil. Remove from the heat and allow to cool fully before placing in the fridge to chill.

Mix together the grapefruit and lemon juices in a bowl. (When squeezing the juice, remove any pips but leave in a little bit of the flesh.) Stir in the elderflower liqueur. Set aside.

Whisk the egg white in another bowl until soft peaks form.

Add the grapefruit and lemon juice mix to the cold lemon-sugar syrup. Fold in the whisked egg white.

Slowly pour the mix into the ice-cream maker and churn for about 40 minutes until the sorbet has started to set but is still smooth. Transfer to a freezer-proof container and keep in the freezer until ready to serve.

Photo overleaf →

Jam jam jam

There is nothing like home-made jam and it is easy to make, especially a small quantity. If you are worried about your jam not setting you can use specialist jam sugar, which has added pectin to help it set. I just add a bit of lemon zest and hope for the best.

Makes 1 jar
(300–350g)
—

* 250g fresh or frozen fruit of your choice (I like mixed red berries)
200g caster sugar
grated zest and juice of 1 lemon

For the Red, White and Blue Meringues (page 130), make the jam with blueberries.

Place a small side plate in the freezer.

If you're using larger fruit such as plums or peaches, chop up and remove stones. Remove stones from cherries too. (Weigh 250g once you've done this.) Put the fresh or frozen fruit, sugar, and lemon zest and juice in a heavy-based saucepan set on a low heat. Stir occasionally until the sugar has dissolved. Turn the heat up and allow the jam to boil for 10 minutes, stirring every so often.

Now test the jam to see if it will set. Take the plate out of the freezer and remove the pan from the heat. Dot some of the hot jam on the plate and leave for a few seconds, then run your finger through the jam. If the surface wrinkles the jam is ready. If the jam isn't ready, return to the heat and boil for another few minutes, then repeat the testing process.

Allow the jam to cool before using in my Cornflake Tart (page 97) or pouring into a sterilised jar and sealing. Store in the fridge for up to a month.

Sticky red onion chutney

This is such a simple and lovely recipe – there really is no need for shop-bought red onion chutney! The red chilli adds a lovely little kick to the sweetness of the red onions but if heat isn't your thing then simply leave it out! This chutney is the perfect accompaniment to my Ham Hock and Chorizo Scotch Eggs (page 171). Slap it on and enjoy. It is also fab with melted Camembert and home-made bread.

Makes 1 jar
—
4 red onions
1 small fresh red chilli (optional)
1 tbsp olive oil
2 fresh thyme sprigs
knob of unsalted butter
100g dark soft brown sugar
100ml balsamic vinegar

Finely chop the red onions and the chilli if using (remove seeds for less heat). Tip into a large heavy-based frying pan and add the olive oil, thyme sprigs and butter. Fry on a medium heat for about 20 minutes until softened, stirring occasionally.

Add the sugar and balsamic vinegar and stir in, then simmer for a further 15–20 minutes until thick, dark and sticky, stirring occasionally.

Remove the thyme sprigs and allow to cool. Pack into a sterilised jar and seal. Store in the fridge and use within a month.

Mango curd

I love mango, and mango curd is rich, sweet and buttery. It's great with ice cream, piled on a Pavlova (see recipe on page 127), used to fill a roulade, spread on toast or just eaten with a spoon! Try swirling through some passion fruit flesh for a bit of extra sharpness and texture.

Makes 600–700ml
—
450g fresh ripe mangoes
grated zest and juice of 2 limes
125g golden caster sugar
125g unsalted butter
4 egg yolks

Peel the mangoes and remove the large stone in the centre. Put the flesh in a food processor and blitz to a purée. Press the purée through a sieve into a heatproof bowl.

Add the remaining ingredients and mix together. Set the bowl over a pan of simmering water and stir constantly until the curd thickens enough to coat the back of the spoon. Allow to cool.

Keep in a clean, covered container in the fridge for up to a week.

Passion fruit curd

Sweet, smooth and tangy, my favourite flavour curd. Use it to fill Pavlova, a roulade or a layered sponge, or just spoon it over vanilla ice cream. When you have a good curd recipe the possibilities are endless.

Makes about 250ml

—

4 large egg yolks
150g golden caster sugar
12 ripe, wrinkled passion fruits
100g unsalted butter

Whisk together the egg yolks and sugar in a mixing bowl for 1 minute.

Scoop out all the flesh and seeds from 10 of the passion fruits into a food processor. Blitz for 10 seconds to loosen the seeds, then press through a sieve into the egg and sugar mix (discard the seeds left in the sieve). Set aside.

Melt the butter in a heavy-based medium-sized saucepan without letting it come to the boil. Add the yolk/fruit mixture and cook over low/medium heat, whisking constantly, until the mixture begins to thicken. This will take about 5 minutes. Don't let it boil!

Off the heat, add the flesh and seeds from the two remaining passion fruits and stir to mix. Pour into a shallow tray and allow to cool. Store in a sterilised jar in the fridge for up to a week.

*To sterilise your jars, wash them (and their lids) in hot, soapy water then let them dry out in a hot oven before filling and sealing.

Being born in North London I was brought up on the pie tradition, in particular pie, mash and liquor (my Dad always had a side of jellied eels too – not something I was keen to include in this book). Pies are so versatile. They can be big, rich and homely or a little more delicate. They can be savoury or sweet and come in all shapes and sizes. All over the world people have made the humble pie their own with different fillings and pastries or doughs and all kinds of shapes (I know – I have tried quite a few!). The range of pies in this chapter makes me smile, and I love each and every one.

This chapter also has recipes for big show-off Sunday lunches and for easy-to-prepare but really tasty dinners. And I had to include two of my most favourite things, namely pork scratchings and sausage rolls with black pudding. The sausage rolls are so popular with my family that they barely make it out of the kitchen before they are devoured.

Savoury bakes, bites & soups

Stilton twisted straws

This recipe makes double the pastry that you need for the cheese straws, so if you prefer you can halve the ingredient quantities. But as it is quite a lot of effort to go to, I think it's worth making the whole amount of pastry and then halving it before adding the Stilton. You can either freeze the other half or keep it in the fridge to use to top a pie, such my Cheese and Onion Pie (page 202). Try to keep everything cold when making pastry – it ensures those all-important layers.

Makes 25—30
—

150g plain flour,
    plus extra for dusting
150g strong white
    bread flour
1 tsp dried thyme
50g lard, cubed
150ml cold water
200g cold unsalted butter
150g Stilton cheese
beaten egg, for egg wash
25g sesame seeds
25g poppy seeds
rock salt
salt and freshly ground
    black pepper

Sift both types of flour into a large bowl and stir in the thyme and a pinch each of salt and pepper. Add the lard and rub in with your fingertips until the mixture resembles breadcrumbs. Stir in the cold water and bring together with your hands to make a dough.

Turn out on to a lightly floured work surface and knead briefly until smooth. Wrap in cling film and chill for 30 minutes.

Remove the dough from the fridge and roll out away from you on the floured surface to a rectangle about 20 x 40cm.

Place the cold butter between two pieces of greaseproof paper and bash/roll with a rolling pin to make a 15 x 25cm rectangle that is about 3mm thick.

Lay the butter rectangle on the bottom two-thirds of the dough – there should be a clear border of about 1cm at the bottom and 2.5cm at the sides. Fold the top third (without butter) down over the middle third, then fold the bottom third up over the middle third (you will now have alternating layers of dough, butter, dough, butter, dough). Pinch the edges together, then chill for 30 minutes.

Remove the dough from the fridge and place on the floured surface so a short side is nearest to you. Roll out away from you to a 20 x 40cm rectangle again. This time fold both the top and bottom of the rectangle in so they meet in the middle, then fold over in half like a book. Pinch the edges together. Chill for 30 minutes.

Place the dough on the floured surface so a short side is nearest to you and roll out away from you to a rectangle again. Fold the top third down over the middle third, then fold the bottom third up over this. Wrap and chill for 30 minutes. Repeat this rolling and folding into thirds three more times with a 30-minute chilling in between each.

Cut the pastry in half. You need just one half for the straws. The other half can be wrapped and kept in the fridge or freezer, to use for my Beef and Ale Pies (page 186), for example. Take the half you are using and roll it out away from you to a rectangle 8–10mm thick. Crumble a quarter of the Stilton on to the middle third of the pastry rectangle, then fold the top third down on top of it. Sprinkle another quarter of Stilton on top of this, then fold the bottom third up over the cheese. Pinch the edges together and gently roll to flatten slightly. Wrap and chill for 30 minutes.

Repeat the rolling and folding process with the rest of the Stilton.

Preheat the oven to 200°C fan (220°C/425°F/Gas Mark 7). Line two baking sheets with greaseproof paper.

Roll out the dough to a large rectangle about 4mm thick. Using a sharp knife trim the edges to make them straight, then cut into 2.5cm-wide strips. Lift each strip and gently twist it a couple of times so you have a spiral, then place on the baking sheet. Gently push the top and bottom of each strip on to the sheet so it doesn't unravel.

Brush the twists with egg wash. Sprinkle half of the twists with the sesame seeds and the other half with the poppy seeds. Sprinkle all with rock salt. Bake for about 20 minutes until golden and crisp.

Serve with a dip such as my Cheesy Spinach and Artichoke Dip (page 224).

Photo overleaf →

Pork scratchings

I was brought up in a pub so of course I had to include how to make pork scratchings! They are definitely one of those love or hate things. I simply love them. For me, a packet of pork scratchings and a pint of cider is sheer perfection. My whole family loves these insanely crunchy, tasty little morsels. I always try to sneak my Dad a few extra as they are his absolute favourite, just like the crackling on roast pork. I have tried to recreate the 'proper' scratchings you would get in bags from butchers' and I think I have come up with a good 'un. Just mind your teeth!

You might want to open the windows and doors while you cook the pork scratchings as the fat can give off some smoke. It is so worth it though!!

Makes about 50 small pieces

—

400g piece pork skin/rind
25g unsalted butter, softened
1 tbsp fennel seeds
salt and freshly ground black pepper

Preheat the oven to 200°C fan (220°C/425°F/Gas Mark 7).

Pat the pork skin dry using kitchen paper. Rub some salt into the skin, then leave for 20 minutes.

Rub the softened butter all over the skin. Using a sharp knife, slice the pork skin into 1cm strips. Sprinkle with the fennel seeds and some pepper.

Place the strips of seasoned pork skin on a raised rack set over a baking tray/roasting tin. Roast for 25–30 minutes until the pork strips are curled, bubbled golden and dry (the melted fat will be in the tray beneath). You may need to turn the tray during roasting to stop the edges catching. Leave to cool on the rack set over the tray.

← *Photo on previous page*

Venison sausage & red onion toad in the hole

Toad in the hole, sausage toad, whatever you want to call it – this is a really rich treat version. You can make a vegetarian version by swapping the venison sausages for vegetarian sausages, but they will need a little less cooking time. If you can't find juniper berries, fennel seeds are a lovely alternative.

Serves 4

150g plain flour
2 large eggs
240ml whole milk
rapeseed oil
knob of butter
1 large red onion, chopped
6 juniper berries
2 garlic cloves, squashed
1 small bunch fresh
   rosemary sprigs
8 good-quality venison
   sausages
salt and freshly ground
   black pepper

Preheat the oven to 200°C fan (220°C/425°F/Gas Mark 7).

Sift the flour into a large bowl and add some salt and pepper. Make a well in the centre and crack in the eggs. Add the milk. Whisk, gradually drawing in the flour, until the batter is smooth. Set aside for about 30 minutes before using.

Meanwhile, pour enough oil into a high-sided roasting tin to fill it by about a third. Place in the oven to heat up for 20 minutes.

Melt the butter in a large frying pan over a medium/high heat and add the onion, juniper berries, garlic, rosemary and sausages. Fry for about 10 minutes stirring and turning regularly, until the onions start to caramelise and the sausages have started to brown all over.

Very very carefully remove the roasting tin of hot oil from the oven. Spoon the sausages and onion mix into the hot oil, spreading it all out, then place back in the oven. Cook for 10 minutes.

Remove the tin from the oven and very carefully and evenly pour in the batter. Return to the oven and bake for 30–35 minutes until the batter has risen and is golden brown.

Serve hot, with mash (see the Beef and Ale Pies recipe on page 186) and gravy (see the Roast Chicken recipe on page 172).

* Venison sausages are rich and have a gamey flavour, so if you prefer, use pork, beef or even chicken bangers.

Pork & apple pasties

I have been told that the crimping on these make them a 'Devon' pasty because the crimp runs along the top. I just like the shape and it means that with every bite you get filling plus crisp pastry. Pork and apple is one of those combinations that just work. Pork fillet doesn't need to be cooked for very long and is nice and tender against the crisp apple chunks.

Makes 12
—

Pastry:
400g plain flour
2 tsp baking powder
1 tsp salt
1 tsp dried sage
½ tsp smoked paprika
110g unsalted butter
2 egg yolks
110ml cold water
beaten egg, for egg wash

Filling:
500g pork fillet
1 medium floury potato, peeled and finely cubed
1 leek, finely sliced
½ red onion, finely chopped
1 tsp chopped garlic (jarred or fresh)
1 tsp chopped red chilli (jarred or fresh)
1 tbsp chopped fresh sage
1 tsp smoked paprika
½ tsp fennel seeds
100g smoked streaky bacon
unsalted butter
2 Bramley apples, peeled, cored and diced
100ml dry cider
salt and freshly ground black pepper

First make the pastry. Put the flour, baking powder, salt, sage and paprika into a bowl. Add the butter and rub together with your fingertips until you have a mixture that resembles breadcrumbs.

Mix in the egg yolks. Slowly add the water, mixing together with your hands until a ball of dough forms. (Alternatively you can make the pastry in a food processor – put in all the ingredients except the water and blitz to breadcrumbs, then gradually work in the water until a ball of dough forms.) Wrap the dough in cling film and chill for about an hour.

Remove any sinew or tendons from the pork fillet, then cut into small cubes. Tip into a large mixing bowl and add the potato, leek, onion, garlic, chilli, sage, paprika, fennel seeds, and some salt and pepper. Snip the bacon into strips directly into the bowl. Get your hands in and give everything a good mix together. Cover with cling film and set aside so the flavours can mingle.

Melt 25g butter in a small saucepan, add the diced apple and cider, and cook over a low heat until the apples have softened and the mixture is thick and reduced. Set aside.

Preheat the oven to 160°C fan (180°C/350°F/Gas Mark 4). Line a baking tray with greaseproof paper.

Roll out the pastry on a lightly floured work surface to the thickness of a £1 coin. Cut out rounds using a small side plate (about 12cm diameter) as a guide. Scrunch together the pastry trimmings, then roll out and cut out more rounds so you have 12 in all.

Spoon some of the pork filling in the centre of each round and add a small knob of butter on top. Spoon some of the apple mix along the top of the meat filling.

Egg wash the edges of each round, then bring up two opposite sides to meet in the centre over the top of the filling. Gently pinch and crimp the edges together so there are no gaps.

Egg wash all of the shaped pasties and poke a small hole in the top to let steam out. Arrange on the lined baking tray and bake for 35–40 minutes until golden brown. Serve hot.

*There should be enough cider left over for you to have a cold glass while you chomp your way through one of these tasty pasties.

* To make 12 smaller,
bite-sized sausage rolls
cut the filled pastry
across into 2.5cm pieces
instead of 5cm pieces

Black pudding sausage rolls

The one recipe that's guaranteed to cause arguments within my family is these sausage rolls. 'Who's got the biggest one?' 'Who got more?' 'Why haven't you made me these?' They are requested frequently and devoured within seconds! Stornaway black pudding is the best in the world apparently (guess who told me that!) so if you can get hold of some try it in this recipe. These are all about flavour – each bite should have a bit of everything. The flaky pastry is perfect without all the folding and turning of puff pastry. Just make sure your butter and water are really cold!

Makes 6–8 sausage rolls
—
Pastry:
150g unsalted butter, frozen
110g strong white bread flour
110g plain flour, plus extra for dusting
2 tsp dried sage
4–5 tbsp ice-cold water
beaten egg, for glazing
sesame and poppy seeds, for sprinkling

Filling:
400g good-quality pork sausagemeat
100g smoked streaky bacon, finely chopped
1 tbsp finely chopped fresh sage
½ tsp dried thyme
2 shallots, finely chopped
½ tsp smoked paprika
100g chestnut mushrooms, finely chopped
1 tsp finely chopped garlic (jarred or fresh)
1 tsp finely chopped red chilli (jarred or fresh)
1 tsp Worcestershire sauce
150g good-quality black pudding
salt and freshly ground black pepper

First make the pastry. Coarsely grate the butter on to a cold plate (do not handle the grated butter). Return to the freezer or put into the fridge to keep cold.

Sift both types of flour into a large bowl and mix in the dried sage, a pinch of salt and some pepper. Without handling the butter, drop it into the flour mix and, using a blunt knife, mix the grated butter into the flour to coat it all evenly. Sprinkle over 2 tablespoons of ice-cold water and mix in with the knife, then gradually add a further 2–3 tablespoons of water until the mix starts to come together.

Finish mixing to a pastry dough with your hands but do not handle the pastry too much. If you need more water add it a couple of drops at a time. The pastry should leave the sides of the bowl clean.

Flatten the pastry into a square shape and wrap it in cling film. Leave to rest in the fridge for 30–45 minutes.

Meanwhile, make the filling. Put all of the filling ingredients, except the black pudding, into a large bowl, with some salt and pepper. Start mixing with a large spoon – then I like to get my hands in and squish it altogether. Fry off a small piece of the filling in a small pan to check the seasoning. Add more to taste. Cover and set aside until needed.

Remove the black outer coating from the black pudding and cut the pudding into 1cm sticks.

Continued overleaf

Continued...

Set the chilled pastry on a lightly floured surface and roll out into a 60 x 30cm rectangle that is about 3mm thick. (If this is too big for your work surface, cut the pastry block in half and roll out each half into a 30 x 15cm oblong piece.) Turn the pastry as you roll to stop it from springing back. As you work, try not to handle the pastry too much.

Trim the edges of the pastry rectangle so they are straight and neat. Spoon the sausagemeat filling into the centre of the pastry and squeeze it together to make a sausage shape that runs across the pastry rectangle, parallel to the 30cm sides (I find flouring your hands helps to do this). Push the sticks of black pudding into the filling in straight lines from end to end.

With cold, floured hands, lift one 30cm side of the pastry up to the middle over the sausage filling and brush the outside edge with beaten egg (or milk). Lift the opposite side of the pastry up to slightly overlap and gently squeeze the edges together to create a sealed join of pastry. Roll the whole thing over so the join is on the bottom. Lift on to a tray and place in the freezer to chill for 10 minutes.

Remove from the freezer and, using a sharp knife, cut across into 5cm pieces. Arrange these, with the join underneath, on a greased baking sheet that has been lined with greaseproof paper. Return to the freezer to keep cold while you preheat the oven to 180°C fan (200°C/400°F/Gas Mark 6).

Glaze the pastry with beaten egg (or milk) and snip a small 'V' on top of each roll. Bake for 20–30 minutes until the pastry is golden brown and the sausage filling is cooked and no longer pink.

Remove from the oven and gently lift the sausage rolls from the baking sheet on to a wire rack to cool.

These taste great with my Sticky Red Onion Chutney (page 154) dolloped on top!

* If you're not keen on black pudding, swap it for sticks of apple or chorizo or, just keep it simple and have nothing at all except sausagemeat.

Ham hock & chorizo Scotch eggs

This is my quite different but very tasty version of the Scotch egg.
The ham hock adds texture and an almost bacon-like flavour that
complements the egg beautifully. As all the elements are already cooked,
the whole thing does not have to be deep-fried for long. So served warm,
the chorizo melts into the ham and the egg yolk is perfectly runny.

Makes 4

—

4 eggs
300g cooked ham hock,
    shredded
60g thinly sliced chorizo,
    chopped
1 small bunch of fresh
    flat-leaf parsley,
    chopped
2 spring onions, finely
    sliced
½ tsp hot smoked paprika
2 eggs, separated
5 slices stale granary
    bread
50g mixed seeds
    (sunflower, pumpkin,
    sesame and pine nuts)
rapeseed oil, for frying
salt and freshly ground
    black pepper

Bring a large saucepan of water to the boil, add the whole eggs and cook
for 5–6 minutes (5 minutes for runny egg yolk; 6 minutes for firmer).

Drain the eggs, then run cold water over them in the pan for a couple
of minutes to stop the cooking. Leave the eggs to sit in the cold water
until you are ready to peel them (the cold water will help prevent the
skin and shell from sticking).

Combine the shredded ham hock, chorizo, parsley and spring onions in
a bowl. Sprinkle over the paprika and salt and pepper to taste, and mix.
(You can taste for seasoning as all of the ingredients are cooked.) Add the
egg yolks and mix again – get your hands in and give the mixture a good
squeeze to make sure everything is well combined.

Blitz the bread slices in a food processor to make breadcrumbs,
then tip them on to a plate. Tip the seeds into the processor and
pulse briefly into uneven pieces that are slightly bigger than the
breadcrumbs. Add these to the breadcrumbs and mix together.

Peel the eggs. Divide the ham hock mix into four portions and mould one
around each egg. Make sure there are no gaps in the ham hock layer and
that you have an evenly shaped ball. Squeeze together gently to seal.

Roll the ham hock-covered egg in the egg whites, then the breadcrumb
and seed mix to coat all over. Repeat this dipping process a second time
to get a good covering.

Heat rapeseed oil in a medium-sized saucepan or deep-fat fryer (three-
quarters full) until it reaches about 180°C (356°F). To check the
temperature without a thermometer, drop a cube of bread into the hot
oil; if it is at/near 180°C the bread cube should bubble, float and turn
golden in about a minute.

Carefully lower two of the Scotch eggs into the hot oil and fry for 3–4
minutes, turning so all sides are cooked, until the breadcrumb coating is
golden and crisp. Remove with a slotted spoon and set on some kitchen
paper to absorb excess oil. Fry the remaining Scotch eggs in the same way.

Serve hot – the ham will be hot, the breadcrumbs crisp and the egg yolk
gorgeous and runny. Try with my Sticky Red Onion Chutney (page 154).

Family roast chicken with all the trimmings

Probably the nation's favourite Sunday roast – chicken – with crisp roast potatoes, Yorkshire puddings to mop up the tasty gravy, bread sauce (Mam always had to make extra to save arguments!) and lots of vegetables. Most components can be prepared while the chicken is cooking or resting, except for the cauliflower cheese, which needs to be cooked at a slightly different temperature. If you don't have a second oven then simply prepare ahead and warm through before serving.

Serves 4–6

½ lemon
1 fresh bouquet garni
   (sage, thyme and
   parsley)
1 large free-range chicken,
   about 2kg
½ onion, chopped
1 leek, trimmed and cut
   in half
½ carrot, chopped
25g unsalted butter,
   softened
3 garlic cloves, cut in half

Roast potatoes:
400g Maris Piper potatoes
1 tbsp plain flour
50g goose fat
rapeseed oil

Swede and carrot mash with cumin:
1 tsp cumin seeds
250g peeled swede, diced
250g peeled carrots, diced
knob of butter

Preheat the oven to 190°C fan (210°C/420°F/Gas 6/7).

Stick the lemon half and bouquet garni up the chicken's bottom. Spread the chopped onion, leek and carrot in a roasting tin and set the chicken on top of the vegetables. Rub the butter all over the chicken and push the garlic cloves under the skin. Massage down so the butter is spread evenly. Sprinkle the chicken with salt and pepper.

Roast for 1¼–1½ hours. Baste the chicken halfway through cooking. The chicken is cooked when the juices run clear (test with the tip of a knife in the thickest part of the bird). Lift the chicken on to a carving board, cover with foil and allow to rest.

While the chicken is roasting, prepare the accompaniments. First get the potatoes ready. Put them in a pan of lightly salted water, bring to the boil and cook until softened. Drain well, then return to the pan and shake around so the edges of the potatoes are roughened. Sprinkle with the flour and leave to dry.

Place the goose fat and a glug of rapeseed oil in a roasting tin and place in the oven (with the chicken) to heat up. Once the fat is hot, carefully add the cooled and fluffy potatoes, spreading them out. Return the pan to the oven and roast for 35–40 minutes until the potatoes are crisp and golden on the outside. Shuffle them around halfway through the cooking.

Meanwhile, prepare the swede and carrot mash. Gently toast the cumin seeds in a dry frying pan for 3–4 minutes. Set aside. Cook the swede and carrot in slightly salted boiling water for about 20 minutes until soft. Drain well, then return to the pan with the butter and toasted cumin seeds and mash together. Season with salt and pepper. Keep hot (or reheat for serving).

Bread sauce:
500ml whole milk
1 onion, halved
1 bay leaf
1 garlic clove, peeled
freshly grated nutmeg
4 slices white bread
  (3 slices blitzed to
  breadcrumbs, 1 torn
  into chunks)

Gravy:
white wine
2 tbsp plain flour
500ml chicken stock
salt and freshly ground
  black pepper

Greens:
100g pumpkin seeds
50g sesame seeds
400g spring greens,
  chopped

And...
One-cup Sage and Onion
  Yorkshire Puddings
  (page 178)
Decadent Cauliflower
  Cheese (page 177)

For the bread sauce, put the milk, onion, bay leaf, garlic and a grating of nutmeg in a saucepan and heat until it starts to boil. Allow to cool, then strain and return to the pan. Add all the bread and some seasoning. Slowly heat up, stirring, until thickened. Keep hot (or reheat for serving).

Once the chicken is out of the oven and resting, you can make the Yorkshire Puddings (see page 178).

To make the gravy, skim off the fat from the chicken juices in the roasting tin. Pour the juices into a saucepan along with the vegetables in the tin and add a good glug of wine and the flour. Bring to the boil, stirring, and stir until thickened. Stir in the stock and boil until reduced slightly. Strain through a sieve into a clean pan, pressing down on all the vegetables in the sieve so you get maximum flavour. If you want a thicker gravy, you can reduce it further. Add seasoning to taste.

For the greens, lightly toast the pumpkin and sesame seeds in a dry frying pan for 3–4 minutes. Set aside. Cook the greens in lightly salted boiling water for 4–5 minutes. Drain, then toss with the toasted seeds. Keep hot.

Carve the chicken and serve with the roast potatoes, Yorkshire puddings, cauliflower cheese, swede and carrot mash, greens, bread sauce and lashings of gravy.

*To get extra flavour from the roasting tin, deglaze the roasting tin with some of the wine and scrape the bottom after pouring the roasting juices into a saucepan, adding them to the saucepan with the rest of the wine.

Photo overleaf →

*For an alternative veg option, fry some broccoli florets in a frying pan with a little toasted sesame oil, Chinese 5-spice and sesame seeds until tender.

Decadent cauliflower cheese

If my Mam ever asked me what I wanted for dinner I would always say cauliflower cheese. It's so homely and comforting. I have come up with this insanely decadent, luxurious, all-singing-and-dancing version, with a creamy blue cheese, bacon, leek and crunchy topping. It is pretty much a meal in itself but can also be a fab addition to a Sunday roast, and will cause arguments over who gets the biggest portion. I don't like wasting food so I use the leaves on a cauliflower too – they are so flavoursome and have a lovely texture.

Serves 4 as a side dish, 2 as a main dish

—

1 large cauliflower
2 leeks, trimmed
  and chopped
100g smoked streaky
  bacon, chopped
1 tsp finely chopped garlic
  (jarred or fresh)
knob of butter
olive oil

Sauce :
50g unsalted butter
50g plain flour
600ml whole milk
2 tsp wholegrain mustard
* 150g Cambozola cheese
salt and freshly ground
  black pepper

Topping :
1 slice granary bread
1 small bunch fresh
  parsley
1 garlic clove, peeled

Preheat the oven to 200°C fan (220°C/425°F/Gas Mark 7).

Remove the leaves from the cauliflower and wash them thoroughly, then chop into 5cm pieces. Break up the head into florets. Place the florets in a large saucepan of boiling water and cook for about 10 minutes until just tender. Add the leaves for the last 3–4 minutes. Drain.

Put the leeks, streaky bacon and garlic in a frying pan with the butter and a glug of olive oil. Fry over a medium heat, stirring occasionally, until the leeks are soft and the bacon has started to crisp up.

Spread the cauliflower (florets and leaves) in an ovenproof dish about 20 x 28cm. Scatter over the leek and bacon mixture and mix through evenly.

To make the sauce, put the butter in a medium saucepan over a low heat. When the butter has melted, add the flour and cook for about 1 minute, stirring. Whisk in the milk in a continuous stream. Keep stirring until the sauce has thickened nicely and will coat the back of a spoon. Add the wholegrain mustard and season with salt and pepper.

Either chop or break up the Cambozola, then add it to the sauce and stir through. Pour the sauce over the cauliflower mix, covering evenly.

Blitz up the bread, parsley and garlic in a food processor to make fine breadcrumbs. Sprinkle this over the cauliflower cheese. Bake for 25–30 minutes until the top is crunchy and golden and the cheese sauce bubbling.

* If you don't like blue cheese or you are preggo, simply substitute a mix of mature Cheddar and Double Gloucester for the Cambozola.

One-cup sage & onion Yorkshire puddings

Everyone needs a go-to Yorkshire pudding recipe and this is mine. It was taught to me by Liam's mum, Beth. She used a teacup full of flour and one of milk with an egg and a little seasoning, and this works every single time. I've added sage and onion as they are staple Sunday roast flavours for me and work perfectly in this simple recipe. The batter is thicker than usual, which means you can get a good stodgy bottom – my idea of heaven, all the better to mop up gravy with. The best part of a Sunday roast.

*These are perfect with roast chicken, but if you are having beef add 2 teaspoons of hot horseradish sauce and some chopped fresh thyme to the batter instead of the onion and sage.

Makes 6–8

—

150g plain flour
I large egg
200ml whole milk
rapeseed oil
I red onion, sliced
I heaped tbsp roughly
  chopped fresh sage
salt and freshly ground
  black pepper

Sift the flour into a large bowl and add some salt and pepper. Make a well in the centre and crack in the egg. Add the milk. Whisk the egg and milk together, then gradually whisk in the flour until you have a smooth, lump-free batter. Set aside for about 30 minutes.

Meanwhile, preheat the oven to 200°C fan (220°C/425°F/Gas Mark 7).

Put a teaspoon of oil into each hole of an 8- or 12-hole muffin tin (there needs to be enough oil to cover the bottom). Put into the oven to heat up for about 15 minutes.

Carefully remove the hot muffin tin from the oven and put some slices of onion and chopped sage into the now very hot oil in each hole. Return to the oven to cook for about 5 minutes until the onion is starting to soften.

Ladle the batter into the holes to fill each about three-quarters full (take care as the oil will be smoking hot). Return the tin to the oven and bake for 20–25 minutes until the puddings are golden and risen. Serve hot.

*I like my Yorkshires with a fair bit of stodge at the bottom so I undercook them slightly, but feel free to play around with batter amounts and cooking time.

Leftover chicken & everything soup

Liam's mum, Beth, inspired this recipe. She always makes soup after a Sunday roast, adding whatever was left over. It was a bit hit and miss with what worked (roast potatoes didn't), but the soup has now become as much of a staple in my house as it is in hers. It's very easy to make and can be frozen in batches for quick (and very healthy) lunches.

Serves 4

—

1 roast chicken carcass
1 chicken stock cube
1 leek, trimmed and finely chopped
1 carrot, peeled and finely chopped
handful of button mushrooms, finely chopped
1 Maggi seasoning cube
100g pearl barley
1 tsp chopped garlic (jarred or fresh)
1 tsp chopped red chilli (jarred or fresh)
1 tsp dried tarragon
1/2 tsp onion salt
150g frozen spinach
pinch of cayenne pepper
1/4 tsp smoked paprika
salt and freshly ground black pepper

Remove any skin from the chicken carcass, then place the carcass in a saucepan with the stock cube and about 2 litres of water to just cover it. Set over a low heat and bring to the boil. Put the lid on the pan and leave to simmer away for 1–1 1/2 hours. Allow to cool fully.

Strain the cooled chicken broth into a second saucepan. Pick all the meat off the carcass and add to the broth. Discard the bones, gristle etc.

Add the leek, carrot and mushrooms to the broth along with the Maggi seasoning cube, pearl barley, garlic and chilli. Sprinkle in the tarragon and onion salt. Set over a medium heat and bring to the boil, then cover, reduce the heat to low and allow to bubble away for up to an hour until the pearl barley is soft (you may want to add a little more water during the cooking time, depending on how thick you like your soup).

About 10 minutes before the end of the cooking time, add the frozen spinach, cayenne pepper and paprika and stir to mix. Keep stirring to break up the spinach as it thaws.

Season with salt and pepper to taste. Serve immediately or allow to cool fully and then freeze.

*You can add just about anything to this soup — whatever vegetables you have in your fridge or freezer (broccoli, cauliflower, greens, sweetcorn, potatoes are all good) — and you can use brown rice, lentils or even orzo instead of pearl barley.

Chicken stew with pesto & pine nut dumplings

Stew and dumplings is one of my favourite meals, comfort food at its best. This is my version with a little Mediterranean twist. Pesto, pine nuts and the hidden mozzarella centres in the dumplings make a lovely little surprise with the tender and tasty chicken. This is a really versatile dinner that will use up all of those vegetables lurking in the fridge.

Serves 4

8–10 skinless chicken
   thigh fillets
1 tbsp plain flour
olive oil
1 large leek, trimmed
   and sliced
1 red onion, chopped
1 green pepper, seeded
   and diced
200g smoked streaky
   bacon, chopped
1 large carrot, peeled
   and chopped
2 celery sticks, chopped
150g mushrooms,
   quartered
1 butternut squash,
   peeled and diced
2 tsp chopped garlic
   (jarred or fresh)
1 tsp dried parsley
1 tsp smoked paprika
100ml white wine
400ml chicken stock

Preheat the oven to 160°C fan (180°C/350°F/Gas Mark 4).

Put the chicken thighs in a large bowl. Sprinkle over the flour and season with salt and pepper. Toss together to coat the chicken in the flour.

Heat a glug of olive oil in a large frying pan over a medium heat. In batches, brown the chicken all over in the hot oil. As each batch is browned, remove from the pan and place in a large casserole dish (it must have a lid). Set the chicken aside.

Add another glug of oil to the frying pan, then add the leek, onion, green pepper, bacon, carrot, celery, mushrooms and butternut squash. Stir around for a minute or so before adding the garlic, then cook for about 5 minutes until everything starts to soften. Tip the softened vegetables into the casserole and add the dried parsley and paprika.

Pour the wine into the frying pan and let it bubble away for a couple of minutes, scraping up and dissolving the bits stuck to the bottom of the pan. Pour the wine into the casserole. Mix everything together before pouring over the chicken stock. You should just be able to see the stock through the chicken and vegetables. Put the lid on the casserole and place it in the oven to cook for about 45 minutes.

Meanwhile, make the dumplings. Mix the flour and suet in a large bowl. Stir through the parsley, pine nuts and Parmesan. Add the pesto and mix in with a spoon, then slowly add cold water, a teaspoon at a time, using your hands to bring everything together until the mixture forms a soft dough (6–7 teaspoons should be enough).

Dumplings:
150g self-raising flour
50g suet
1 tbsp chopped fresh
    flat-leaf parsley
50g pine nuts
50g Parmesan, freshly
    grated
1 tsp green pesto
    (jarred or home-made)
100g mozzarella
salt and freshly ground
    black pepper

Cut the mozzarella into small cubes. Divide the dough into eight equal portions and shape each into a ball, pushing a cube of mozzarella into the middle.

Remove the stew from the oven and taste for seasoning – if needed, add salt and pepper and a little more paprika. Gently sit the dumplings on top of the hot stew. Replace the lid and put back in the oven to cook for a further 30 minutes.

Remove from the oven and take the lid off – the dumplings should be puffed and have soaked up the gorgeous juices from the stew. It's fine on its own, but you can serve with mash and Savoy cabbage if you like.

* If you're a fan of tomatoes, tear up 50g of sun-dried tomatoes and add these to the stew. You can also leave out the pesto, in which case you may need an extra splash of water to bring the dumplings together.

Roasted red pepper, squash & sweet potato soup

There is nothing quite like a bowl of hot soup with a chunk of home-made bread on a cold day. The bread needs to be slathered in salted butter before dunking it into the hot soup! I find roasting the vegetables instead of boiling them adds a lovely deep flavour.

Serves 4

300g peeled and chopped
   sweet potato
300g peeled and chopped
   butternut squash
   (seeds removed)
2 large red peppers,
   quartered and seeded
1 tsp chopped garlic
   (jarred or fresh)
1 small red chilli, seeded
   and chopped
1 tsp hot smoked paprika
1/2 tsp dried basil
olive oil
1/4 tsp cayenne pepper
500ml vegetable stock
   (stock cube and boiling
   water is fine)
1 tbsp mixed seeds
   (sunflower, pumpkin,
   sesame, poppy, pine
   nuts)
shavings of Parmesan
   cheese
1 small bunch fresh basil
salt and freshly ground
   black pepper

Preheat the oven to 160°C fan (180°C/350°F/Gas Mark 4).

Put the sweet potato, butternut squash and red peppers in a baking tray/roasting tin. Mix in the garlic and chilli, then sprinkle over the paprika and dried basil. Add a good glug of olive oil and mix together.

Roast the vegetables for 45–60 minutes, stirring them round every 15 minutes, until they are soft. (If the edges start to catch, cover with foil.)

Remove from the oven, cover the tray with foil and leave for 10–15 minutes (this helps create steam, which will make it easier to remove the skin from the red peppers).

Peel the skin from the red peppers and discard. Tip all the softened vegetables into a large pan (or a food processor) and add the cayenne pepper. Pour in the stock and blitz with a hand blender (or in the processor) until smooth. Taste and add salt and pepper as desired. Depending on how thick you like your soup you may need to add some water.

Toast the mixed seeds in a dry frying pan over a medium heat. Roughly chop the fresh basil.

Reheat the soup in a saucepan, if needed, and serve with a sprinkle of shaved Parmesan, a few toasted seeds and some basil. If you are feeling decadent you could add a swirl of cream to each bowlful before serving.

A match made in heaven is this soup with a chunk of my warm buttery Mediterranean Soda Bread (page 214).

Beef & ale pies, mash & liquor

I love a pie. It's in my blood – I suppose it's a London thing! You can use any cut of beef for this comforting pie. It is cooked for hours so breaks down any tough cuts. Suet pastry makes a lovely change from puff and is robust enough to hold and soak up some of the wonderful juices from the beef. You don't need the liquor but it's a fab alternative to gravy and makes me feel right at home.

Makes 4 (serves 4–8)
—

Beef filling:
800g beef shin
75g plain flour
1 tsp salt
1 tbsp rapeseed oil
40g unsalted butter
1 large red onion, chopped
1 large leek, trimmed and
   chopped
200g chestnut
   mushrooms, chopped
2 celery sticks, chopped
2 tsp chopped garlic
   (jarred or fresh)
1 fresh bouquet garni
   (rosemary, thyme,
   parsley)
1 tbsp tomato purée
1 tsp smoked paprika
2 tsp dried rosemary
1 tsp dried sage
250ml stout
250ml fresh beef stock
2 red Romano peppers,
   seeded and chopped
2 large carrots, chopped

Cut away any sinew or tendons from the meat, then chop it into bite-sized chunks.

Combine the flour, salt and some pepper on a plate and mix together. Toss the beef chunks in the seasoned flour to coat lightly.

Heat the oil in a heavy-based saucepan or flameproof casserole until almost smoking hot. Working in batches, add the flour-coated chunks of beef and brown on all sides. As each batch is browned, remove with a slotted spoon and place on a plate.

Add the butter to the pan along with the onion, leek, mushrooms, celery, garlic and bouquet garni. Cook for 6–8 minutes until the vegetables are soft, stirring occasionally.

Return the browned beef chunks to the pan with any juices from the plate. Add the tomato purée and stir in, then sprinkle over the paprika, dried herbs and some salt and pepper.

Pour in the stout and stir well. Allow to bubble for 1–2 minutes before adding the beef stock and mixing. Bring to the boil, then turn down to a simmer, cover with a lid and leave to cook for 3 hours.

Add the red peppers and carrots and stir them in. If the mixture looks dry, add more stock. Put the lid back on and simmer for a further hour until the meat is tender enough to melt in the mouth. Check the seasoning and add salt and pepper to taste. Allow the filling to cool.

While the beef filling is simmering, make the pastry. Put the flour, suet, parsley, and a pinch each of salt and pepper in a large bowl and mix together. Grate the frozen butter into the flour mix. Use a table knife to toss together, coating the strands of butter with the seasoned flour. Make a well in the centre and pour in some of the water. Mix with the flour and fat using the knife, adding more water as needed to bring the mixture together. Knead just to make a smooth dough, but do not handle the dough too much. Wrap in cling film and keep in the fridge until needed.

Feeling brave? Dad would always have a side of jellied eels with his pie and mash!

Pastry:
225g plain flour, plus extra
    for dusting
85g beef suet
1 ½ tsp dried parsley
60g frozen unsalted butter
150ml cold water
beaten egg, for egg wash

Mash:
400g fluffy potatoes,
    peeled
big knob of butter
whole milk
double cream

Liquor:
50g unsalted butter
25g cornflour
500ml fresh chicken stock
1 big handful of fresh
    parsley sprigs, chopped
1 tsp finely chopped garlic
    (jarred or fresh)
salt and freshly ground
    black pepper

Preheat the oven to 180°C fan (200°C/400°F/Gas Mark 6).

Divide the cooled beef filling between four individual pie tins that measure about 15 x 10cm, with rims.

Lightly flour a work surface and roll out the pastry to 4–5mm thick. Cut out 4 lids for the pies – they should be slightly bigger than the pie tins. Egg wash the rim of each pie tin, then gently lay the pie lid on top. Use a fork to press down the edge and stick the pastry to the rim of the tin.

Egg wash the pie lids, then use a sharp knife to make a little cut in the centre of each to let steam out during baking. Place in the oven and bake for 25–30 minutes until the pastry is golden and crisp and the juices of the filling are just bubbling around the edges – dribbles are fine!

Meanwhile, make the mash. Cook the potatoes in a pan of lightly salted boiling water for about 20 minutes until really soft. Drain well and return to the pan. Add the butter, a splash of milk and a glug of double cream. Mash until your arm hurts, then beat in salt and pepper to taste. (If you are feeling fancy, you could also add some grated cheese and chopped spring onions too.)

Make the liquor while the potatoes are cooking. Melt the butter in a saucepan, add the cornflour and mix to a smooth paste. Gradually whisk in the stock and bring to a simmer, still whisking. Add the parsley and garlic and keep stirring until smooth and slightly thickened. Season to taste.

Serve the pies hot, in their tins, with a healthy dollop of mash and the liquor poured over.

Photo overleaf →

Vegetable quiche

My Mam makes a great quiche that is jam-packed with everything. In fact, it's one of the things Liam will ask her to make for him (and she always does!). This is my attempt to make a quiche that's as good as hers. It is vegetarian but the meaty mushrooms and thick-sliced courgettes make it very satisfying, and salty feta cheese gives it a lovely tangy flavour.

Serves 6

Roast vegetables:
1 green pepper, seeded
    and diced
150g mushrooms, sliced
200g courgettes, sliced
1 tsp chopped garlic
    (jarred or fresh)
1 tsp chopped red chilli
    (jarred or fresh)

Pastry:
200g plain flour
1 tsp dried parsley
100g cold unsalted butter
1 egg yolk
3–4 tbsp cold water
beaten egg, for egg wash

Filling:
4 eggs
120ml double cream
120ml whole milk
3 spring onions, chopped
1 tbsp chopped fresh flat-
    leaf parsley
½ tsp smoked paprika
150g feta cheese, crumbled
8 cherry tomatoes,
    cut in half
50g Parmesan, freshly
    grated
25g pine nuts
salt and freshly ground
    black pepper

Preheat the oven to 160°C fan (180°C/350°F/Gas Mark 4).

Put the pepper, mushrooms, courgettes, garlic, chilli and some seasoning in a baking tray. Toss together, then spread out. Roast for about 20 minutes, stirring once. Allow to cool. Leave the oven on.

While the vegetables are roasting, make the pastry. Put the flour, dried parsley and a pinch each of salt and pepper into a large bowl and mix together. Add the cubed butter and rub in with your fingertips until the mixture resembles breadcrumbs. (Or blitz it all together in a food processor.) Add the egg yolk, then slowly mix in enough of the cold water to bring it all together to make a soft but firm dough (you might not need all of the water). Wrap in cling film and chill for 30 minutes.

Roll out the pastry on a lightly floured surface to about 3mm thick. Drape into a 25cm loose-bottomed fluted tart tin and gently push into the flutes. Prick the pastry case with a fork and chill for 20 minutes.

Crumple up a piece of greaseproof paper, then smooth it out and use to line the pastry case. Fill with baking beans. Bake blind for 20 minutes. Remove the beans and paper, then bake for a further 10 minutes until golden. As soon as you remove the pastry case from the oven, brush the hot pastry base with egg wash. Leave the oven on.

In a large bowl mix together the eggs, cream, milk, spring onions, parsley, paprika and some seasoning.

Layer the courgette, pepper and mushroom mix with the crumbled feta in the pastry case, then fill with the egg mixture and mix lightly together with a fork. Arrange the halved cherry tomatoes on top, cut-side up. Scatter the Parmesan and pine nuts over the tomatoes.

Bake for 35–40 minutes until the filling is firm but still with a slight wobble in the centre. Serve warm with a heap of salad.

Chunky shepherd's pie

I came up with this because a certain Scottish boy of mine decided that he didn't like regular shepherd's pie. He likes mince and he likes potatoes – just not cooked together in the same pot! So I tried it with lamb stewing steak and voilà! The chunky shepherd's pie is now a permanent menu option at home! This is a really rich and decadent dinner, smoky, a little pokey and full of lovely ingredients. The topping is almost a meal in itself but we always have seconds!

Serves 4 hungry people

—

olive oil

1 heaped tbsp plain flour

800g lamb stewing steak (e.g. neck), cut into 50p-sized pieces

1 large red onion, diced

1 red pepper, seeded and diced

3 small carrots, peeled and diced

2 celery sticks, diced

150g chestnut mushrooms, diced

100g chorizo, skinned and sliced

leaves from 1 small bunch fresh rosemary, thyme and sage, finely chopped

1 dried bay leaf

2 tsp finely chopped garlic (jarred or fresh)

1 small fresh red chilli, finely chopped (remove the seeds if you don't like too much heat)

1 tsp hot smoked paprika

½ tsp paprika

½ tsp cayenne pepper

1 tsp dried thyme

Continued overleaf...

Preheat the oven to 160°C fan (180°C/350°F/Gas Mark 4).

Heat up a glug of olive oil in a large frying pan over a medium/high heat. Season the flour with salt and pepper, then toss the lamb in the flour to coat lightly all over. Fry – in batches – until browned on all sides. As each batch of lamb is browned, transfer to a large casserole using a slotted spoon.

Add another glug of olive oil to the frying pan followed by the diced vegetables and sliced chorizo, the fresh herbs, bay leaf, garlic and chilli. Fry for 4–5 minutes until the vegetables are softened, stirring frequently.

Stir in the paprika (both types), cayenne, dried thyme and mushroom powder. Turn the heat to medium. Add the tomato purée and stir in, then pour in the red wine. Allow this to bubble away for a couple of minutes before stirring in the beef stock and Worcestershire sauce. Make sure you get all of the lovely bits off the bottom of the pan.

Tip the whole lot over the meat in the casserole and give it a good mix round. The liquid should just be visible through the top layer of meat. Place the lid on the casserole and transfer to the oven to cook for 2–2½ hours until the meat is tender. Stir occasionally.

With about 1½ hours of cooking time to go, prick the sweet and baking potatoes with a knife, then set them on a baking tray and place in the oven with the casserole to bake for the remaining time.

Continued overleaf →

Continued...

* If you don't want to use lamb then swap it for pork and cook for the same length of time. Or you can use beef casserole chunks but increase cooking time to 3–3½ hours so the meat is really tender.

2 tsp mushroom/
  porcini powder (or
  mushroom ketchup)
1 heaped tbsp tomato
  purée
200ml red wine
300ml beef stock
  (fresh or from stock
  cube)
1 tbsp Worcestershire
  sauce

Topping:
4 sweet potatoes
4 large baking potatoes
milk
butter
3 leeks, trimmed
  and sliced
100g grated cheese
  (I like a mature
  Cheddar)
salt and freshly ground
  black pepper

Melt a knob of butter in a frying pan over a low/medium heat, add the leeks and cook for 5–6 minutes until soft. Set aside to cool.

When the meat filling is cooked, remove the casserole from the oven – the sauce should be rich and thick. Taste for seasoning, add more if needed and stir through. Cover the casserole and set aside. Increase the oven temperature to 180°C fan (200°C/400°F/Gas Mark 6).

Using a sharp knife (holding the potato with a tea towel), cut each sweet and baking potato in half lengthways and scoop out the soft flesh into a large bowl. Mash all the flesh together with a splash of milk and knob of butter. Stir through the leeks and half of the grated cheese. Season with black pepper.

Cover the meat mixture with the potato and cheese mix – I like to pile it on willy-nilly. Scatter the remaining grated cheese over the top. Put the casserole back into the oven (without the lid) and bake for about 25 minutes until the cheese has melted, the top is golden and the meat juices are bubbling up around the edges.

Serve hot, with a heap of broccoli and greens.

* Brushing the pastry case with
  egg wash after it has been baked,
  before adding the filling, acts as a
  seal to help prevent seepage.

Chorizo, pepper & sweet potato tart

Tart? Quiche? Who knows? Whichever, it is yummy! I like to have plenty of filling and a whole heap of cheese so that when eaten warm you get the flavours and textures but also that naughty melted stretch of the cheese on top! I've tried to keep the flavours fairly Spanish with the chorizo, Manchego cheese and paprika but you can change the flavours to anything or any country you want!

Serves 6—8

Filling:
200g sweet potato
2 red Romano peppers
1 red onion, sliced
olive oil
1 tsp chopped garlic
    (jarred or fresh)
1 tsp chopped red chilli
    (jarred or fresh)
1/2 tsp smoked paprika
4 eggs
120ml double cream
120ml whole milk
150g Manchego cheese,
    grated
100g chorizo, skinned
    and diced
1 tbsp chopped fresh basil
50g Parmesan cheese,
    freshly grated
25g pine nuts

Pastry:
200g plain flour
1/2 tsp dried basil
100g cold unsalted
    butter, cubed
1 egg yolk
3–4 tbsp ice-cold water
beaten egg, for egg wash
salt and freshly ground
    black pepper

Preheat the oven to 160°C fan (180°C/350°F/Gas Mark 4).

Peel the sweet potato and slice into 3mm rounds. Cook in a pan of boiling water for about 5 minutes until just soft. Drain and set aside on kitchen paper, in one layer, to dry out.

To make the pastry, combine the flour, dried basil and some salt and pepper in a bowl and mix together. Add the cubed butter and rub in to make a breadcrumb texture. (Or put all the ingredients in a food processor and blitz until they start to come together.) Mix in the egg yolk and enough cold water, 1 tablespoon at a time, to make a soft but firm pastry.

Roll out the pastry on a lightly floured surface to about 3mm thickness and lay into a 25cm round loose-bottomed tin, lining the tin smoothly and pushing in the pastry 'corners'. Prick the pastry case with a fork, then chill for 20 minutes.

Meanwhile, remove the seeds from the red peppers and slice into strips. Mix with the red onion in a baking tray and stir through a good glug of olive oil, the garlic, chilli, paprika and some seasoning. Roast for about 15 minutes, stirring halfway through. Remove from the oven and allow to cool.

Scrunch up a piece of baking parchment, then smooth it out and use to line the pastry case. Fill with baking beans and bake blind for 20 minutes. Remove the paper and beans, then bake for a further 10 minutes until the pastry is golden brown.

Meanwhile, in a large bowl mix together the eggs, cream, milk, grated Manchego cheese and some salt and pepper.

Remove the pastry case from the oven (leave the oven on). Brush the pastry base with egg wash, then layer up the sweet potato slices and pepper and onion mix in the case. Scatter the diced chorizo and chopped fresh basil over the top. Pour over the egg and cheese mixture and mix in lightly with a fork. Sprinkle with the Parmesan and pine nuts.

Return to the oven and bake for 35–40 minutes until the filling is firm but still has a slight wobble in the centre. Serve warm or cold.

Choose-your-lid chicken pie

Like anything in life, it's important to have choices – especially when it comes to pies! This recipe gives you the choice of what you put on top of a very thick and tasty chicken filling. Perfect if you have a fussy family or a particular pastry fondness. Pies like this are great for using up vegetables and every last bit of a roast chicken (make a concentrated stock with the carcass and freeze in an ice-cube tray for ready-made stock cubes).

Serves 4–6

—

1 cooked chicken (I use a roast chicken)
knob of unsalted butter
olive oil
2 leeks, trimmed and sliced
150g button mushrooms
200g dry-cure streaky bacon, cut into strips
2 celery sticks, chopped
2 tsp chopped garlic (jarred or fresh)
2 tbsp plain flour
300ml dry cider
200g crème fraîche
2 heaped tsp wholegrain mustard
¼ tsp cayenne pepper
¼ tsp smoked paprika
splash of whole milk
salt and freshly ground black pepper

Choose your lid:

* 200g puff pastry (see Stilton Twisted Straws, page 158, if you want to make your own puff pastry)

* 200g shortcrust pastry (see Chorizo, Pepper and Sweet Potato Tart, page 195)

* 200g flaky pastry (see Black Pudding Sausage Rolls, page 167)

* 200g suet pastry (see Beef and Ale Pies, page 186)

* 8 sheets filo pastry (see Individual Banoffee Pies, page 135, if you want to make your own filo) plus 50g melted butter

Plus:
plain flour for dusting
beaten egg, for egg wash

* This is a perfect after-Christmas pie – use leftover turkey meat and ham instead of chicken and bacon, and add a little cranberry sauce.

Preheat the oven to 190°C fan (210°C/420°F/Gas Mark 6/7).

Strip the chicken meat from the bones and place in a large bowl. (Keep the carcass for making stock or soup.)

Heat the butter with a glug of olive oil in a large saucepan. Add the leeks, button mushrooms (leave them whole), bacon strips, celery and garlic, and cook over a low/medium heat until everything starts to soften and turn a little golden.

Stir through the flour and allow to cook out for a couple of minutes, then gradually stir in the cider and cook for a few more minutes. Add the crème fraîche and wholegrain mustard along with the cayenne pepper and paprika and mix well. Add a splash of milk if the mix is too thick.

Remove from the heat. Add the chicken meat. Season with salt and pepper. Transfer the chicken mixture to a large pie dish with a rim and allow to cool.

If you are using puff, shortcrust, flaky or suet pastry for the lid, dust a work surface with flour, then roll out the pastry to 4–5mm thick and slightly bigger than the ovenproof dish rim. Egg wash the rim, then gently lift the pastry over the filling. Using a fork, crimp the edge of the pastry lid so it sticks to the rim of the dish. Poke or cut a small steam hole in the centre, then egg wash the lid.

If using filo, gently scrunch up the sheets of pastry and place them on top of the pie filling. Brush the visible edges and points of the pastry with melted butter.

Bake the pie for 30–35 minutes (25–30 minutes for filo) until the filling is bubbling and your pastry lid is golden and crisp.

Allow to cool for a few minutes before cutting and serving with buttered new potatoes and spring greens.

Fish pie

This is a dish I make when Liam is out because he isn't a huge fan of what he calls 'fishy fish'. I could eat this every day! Fish pie can be a bit samey in flavour and in texture but this version, with a variety of fish as well as juicy king prawns, soft-boiled eggs and fresh spinach, avoids that. The best bit for me is the melted mozzarella nestled under the double mash.

Serves 4–6

300ml whole milk
300ml double cream
1 tsp dried tarragon
1 dried bay leaf
1 tsp chopped garlic
    (jarred or fresh)
750g filleted sustainable
    fish (I used a mix
    of salmon, smoked
    haddock and pollock)
200g peeled, cooked king
    prawns
3 eggs
100g fresh spinach
75g fresh mozzarella

Sauce:
25g unsalted butter
1 heaped tbsp plain flour
2 heaped tbsp ricotta
1 tbsp finely chopped
    fresh flat-leaf parsley

Topping:
300g sweet potatoes,
    peeled and chopped
300g fluffy white potatoes,
    peeled and chopped
splash of milk
knob of unsalted butter
3 spring onions, chopped
25g Parmesan, grated
salt and freshly ground
    pepper

Mix together the milk, cream, tarragon, bay leaf and garlic in a large pan. Bring to the boil, then reduce the heat to a simmer. Place the fish in the pan and cover with the lid. Leave to cook gently for 5–8 minutes until the fish flakes when nudged with a fork.

Using a slotted spoon, remove the fish from the poaching liquor and place in a bowl to cool. Strain the poaching liquor through a sieve into a jug and set aside.

Once the fish has cooled, remove any skin and break into chunks (discard any bones there may be). Place the mixed fish chunks in an ovenproof dish and scatter the king prawns on top.

Put the eggs into a saucepan of boiling water and boil for 6 minutes. Pour off the boiling water and run cold water over the eggs for 1 minute. Peel the eggs and cut into quarters. Lay these on top of the fish mixture, then scatter the spinach leaves over the surface.

Preheat the oven to 180°C fan (200°C/400°F/Gas Mark 6).

For the topping, cook the sweet and white potatoes in a saucepan of salted boiling water for about 15 minutes until soft. Drain well, then mash together with the milk and butter before folding through the chopped spring onions and seasoning to taste.

Make the sauce while the potatoes are cooking. Melt the butter in a saucepan over a low/medium heat. Stir in the flour and cook, still stirring, for 3–4 minutes. Pour in the strained poaching liquor and stir until the sauce comes to the boil and thickens. Add the ricotta, parsley and pepper to taste and mix well. Pour the sauce over the fish and spinach.

Top with ripped-off pieces of mozzarella and then the mashed potatoes – leave it all lumpy and bumpy and higgledy piggledy. Finally, sprinkle with the Parmesan. Bake for 25–30 minutes until the potato topping is starting to crisp and look golden in places. Serve hot with broccoli and French beans.

Macaroni pies

When we were young, Mam and Dad used to take us to Tomintoul in Scotland round about February time. We used to stay in a lovely little cottage, go on long walks with the dogs and nearly always would welcome snow. One of my favourite things to eat were the macaroni pies that I only ever found in Scotland. Pastry, pasta and cheese – so naughty but so nice, and fine for a little treat now and again. Not many people had heard of them but of course my other half, who is from Scotland, knew all about them and our mutual love of macaroni pies was born. I made these at his request and they are now a family favourite. I hope to spread the macaroni pie love to all – in moderation of course!

Makes 8 small pies

—

Pastry:
40g lard
100g plain flour, plus extra for dusting
75g strong white bread flour
¼ tsp smoked paprika
35g butter

Filling:
200g macaroni
200g dry-cured smoked streaky bacon, chopped
1 tsp chopped garlic (jarred or fresh)
25g unsalted butter
25g plain flour
400ml whole milk
1 tsp Dijon mustard
½ tsp smoked paprika
75g Double Gloucester, grated
100g mature Cheddar, grated
25g Parmesan, freshly grated
salt and freshly ground black pepper

Put the lard in a small saucepan with 70ml water and heat gently until the lard has melted and the water is hot.

Meanwhile, in a large bowl mix together both types of flour, the paprika and a pinch each of salt and pepper. Add the butter and rub it in with your fingertips until the mixture resembles breadcrumbs.

Pour the hot water and lard mix over the flour mix and stir until it all starts to come together. Use your hands to bring it together into a dough and gently knead until smooth. Wrap in cling film and chill while you make the filling.

Add the macaroni to a large saucepan of salted boiling water and boil for about 8 minutes (or according to packet instructions) until tender. Scoop out about 120ml of the pasta water and reserve this, then drain the pasta in a colander. Allow to cool slightly.

Put the bacon and garlic in a dry frying pan over a medium heat and cook until the fat runs and the bacon starts to crisp. Remove from the heat and set aside.

Preheat the oven to 170°C fan (190°C/375°F/Gas Mark 5).

continued overleaf →

Continued...

Using the same large saucepan, melt the butter, stir in the flour and cook over a low heat for 1–2 minutes. Slowly add the milk, stirring the whole time. Turn up the heat slightly and simmer, stirring, until the sauce starts to thicken. Add the mustard, paprika and some salt and pepper and stir through. Add the Double Gloucester and Cheddar and stir through until melted. Finally, stir in the bacon and garlic. If the mixture is looking a little too thick add some of the reserved pasta water. Taste and adjust the seasoning if needed.

Remove the dough from the fridge and roll out on a lightly floured work surface to about 2mm thick. Cut out 8 x 20cm rounds and line the 7.5cm holes in a muffin tin, pushing the dough in gently to line evenly and smoothly. The dough cases should have nice high sides.

Fill the dough cases with the macaroni cheese mix (you will only use about half of it – see below). Sprinkle the grated Parmesan on top. Bake for 25–30 minutes until the pastry is cooked and the filling is golden and crisp on top. Serve hot.

* You will have about half of the macaroni mix left, which can be frozen and then thawed whenever you want to eat it.

To make a dish perfect for a weeknight meal for four, put the macaroni mix in an ovenproof dish and poke in about 6 cherry tomatoes, cut in half. If you like a bit of heat you can scatter over some chopped jalapeños before sprinkling with Parmesan. Bake in a preheated 180°C fan (200°C/400°F/Gas Mark 6) oven for 20–25 minutes.

Cheese & onion pie

When I used to go on holiday to Greece with my parents, I loved to eat the pastries, both sweet and savoury. It's the same now, with Liam. I adore visiting Greek bakeries and tasting the pies, from savoury spanakopita or tiropita to the sweet filo pastries layered with custard or vanilla cream (I once ate so many of these I was sick!). I wanted to create a savoury pie that reminded me of Greek pastries as well as a French galette, which I am also extremely fond of. This is warming, cheesy and very tasty. It works well served hot for dinner or cold sliced on a picnic.

Serves 4 for dinner
—

Pastry:
150g plain flour, plus extra for dusting
150g strong white bread flour
pinch of salt
50g lard, cubed
150ml cold water
200g cold unsalted butter
beaten egg, for egg wash

First make the pastry. Sift both types of flour into a large bowl, then stir in the salt. Add the lard and rub in with your fingertips until the mixture resembles breadcrumbs. Stir in the cold water and bring together with your hands. Turn out the dough on to a lightly floured work surface and knead briefly until smooth. Wrap in cling film and chill for 30 minutes.

Meanwhile, place the cold butter between two pieces of greaseproof paper and bash/roll with a rolling pin until you have a flat 15 x 25cm rectangle that is about 3mm thick.

Roll out the chilled dough on the floured surface (rolling away from you) to a 20 x 40cm rectangle. Lay the butter rectangle on the bottom two-thirds of the dough rectangle. There should be a clear border of about 1cm at the bottom and 2.5cm at the sides.

Fold the top, unbuttered third of the dough rectangle down over the middle third, then fold the bottom third up over the middle third (you will now have alternating layers of dough, butter, dough, butter, dough). Pinch the edges together, then wrap and chill for 30 minutes.

Flour the work surface again and set the dough on it so a short side is nearest to you. Roll out away from you into a 20 x 40cm rectangle again. This time fold both the top and bottom of the rectangle in so they meet in the middle, then fold it in half like a book. Pinch the edges together. Wrap and chill for 30 minutes.

Roll out the dough into a rectangle as before. Fold the top third down and the bottom third up over it. Wrap and chill for 30 minutes. Repeat this rolling and folding process (called a 'turn') three times, chilling in between for 30 minutes. This will make a total of four turns. Keep the dough in the fridge until ready to use.

Now make the filling. Peel the sweet and white potatoes and cut them into 3–4mm slices. Add to a pan of lightly salted boiling water and boil for 5–6 minutes until softened. Drain and set aside.

Filling:
1 sweet potato
1 white potato (about
    the size of the sweet
    potato)
1 red onion, halved
    and sliced
1 white onion, halved
    and sliced
1 bay leaf
knob of unsalted butter
olive oil
1 tsp chopped garlic
    (jarred or fresh)
1 tbsp chopped fresh sage
1 heaped tbsp plain flour
125ml whole milk
50ml double cream
1/2 tsp chilli powder
1/2 tsp nigella seeds
1/2 tsp wholegrain mustard
75g mature Cheddar,
    grated
75g Double Gloucester,
    grated
salt and freshly ground
    black pepper

Put the red and white onions in a frying pan with the bay leaf, butter and a glug of olive oil. Set over a low heat and fry until the onions start to soften. Add the garlic and sage and fry for a further 10–15 minutes until very soft and sweet.

Add the flour to the pan and cook, stirring, for a few minutes. Pour in the milk and stir constantly until the mixture starts to bubble and thicken. Pour in the cream and sprinkle over the chilli and nigella seeds. Finally, stir through the mustard followed by the Cheddar. Set aside.

Preheat the oven to 200°C fan (225°C/425°F/Gas Mark 7). Line a baking sheet with greaseproof paper.

Lightly flour the work surface and roll out the pastry to 3–4mm thick. Using a dinner plate about 30cm in diameter as a guide, cut out a round. Then cut out a second round about 2.5cm smaller than the first.

Place the smaller round on the lined baking sheet. Layer about a third of the potatoes on the smaller round, leaving about a 2.5cm clear border around the edge. Spread about a third of the onion mix over the potatoes, then add a sprinkling of the grated Double Gloucester. Add another layer of potatoes followed by the onion mix and more grated cheese. Repeat the process a third time, finishing with the last of the grated cheese.

Egg wash the pastry border. Gently lift up the bigger round of pastry and lay it over the filling (you may need to roll it out a little more to ensure it fits). Gently tease the edge of the bigger round down so they meet the edge of the egg-washed border, then use your fingers to pinch the edges together or crimp with a fork.

Egg wash the whole pastry lid, then poke three holes or small slits in the top so steam can escape. Sprinkle with salt and pepper. Bake for 35–40 minutes until the pastry is golden and crisp.

Leave the pie to sit for 10–15 minutes before serving warm, or allow to cool completely before slicing.

*If you like blue cheese, swap the two cheeses for creamy Gorgonzola.

Salmon, prawn & asparagus tart

This is like a really posh quiche, packed full of salmon, king prawns and asparagus. I think tarts like these should have more filling than egg mixture and this is a great example of that. Try to use sustainable fish – a lovely alternative to salmon is rainbow trout or even smoked haddock. Just be careful of the seasoning if you use smoked fish.

Serves 6

Filling:
2 x 150g pieces skinless salmon fillet
180g peeled raw king prawns, thawed if frozen
1 tbsp fresh dill
1/2 tsp chilli flakes
1 tsp finely chopped garlic (jarred or fresh)
grated zest of 1 lemon
olive oil
200g fresh asparagus spears
4 eggs
80ml double cream
50g Gruyère, grated
100g Parmesan, freshly grated
beaten egg, for egg wash
salt and freshly ground black pepper
fresh chives, to garnish

Pastry:
250g plain flour, plus extra for dusting
1 tsp dried parsley
125g cold unsalted butter, cubed
2 medium egg yolks
50ml ice-cold water

Preheat the oven to 160°C fan (180°C/350°F/Gas Mark 4).

First start the filling. Make a foil pouch and put in the salmon, prawns, fresh dill, chilli, garlic, lemon zest and a seasoning of salt and pepper. Drizzle over some olive oil and seal the parcel. Place on a baking tray and bake for 12–15 minutes until the salmon will flake when nudged with a fork and the prawns are pink. Remove from the oven, fold open the parcel and leave to cool. Leave the oven on.

To make the pastry, put the flour, dried parsley and a pinch each of salt and pepper into a large bowl and mix together. Add the cubed butter and rub it in with your fingertips until the mixture resembles breadcrumbs.

Drop in the egg yolks and mix in with your hands, then slowly add enough of the cold water to bring together into a dough (you might not need all of the water). Knead lightly just until smooth – do not handle too much – then wrap and chill for about 15 minutes.

Bend each asparagus spear and snap off the woody end. Blanch the asparagus in a pan of boiling salted water for 1 minute. Drain, then slice in half lengthways. Set aside.

Mix together the eggs, double cream and some salt and pepper in a bowl. Add the Gruyère and most of the Parmesan and mix through.

Roll out the pastry on a lightly floured work surface to 3mm thick and use to line a 20 x 24cm rectangular fluted tin with a loose bottom. Crumple up a piece of greaseproof paper, then smooth it out and use to line the pastry case. Fill with baking beans. Bake blind for 15 minutes. Remove the beans and paper. Brush the pastry case with egg wash, then bake for a further 5 minutes until golden brown.

Gently flake the salmon into chunks and spread in the pastry case. Arrange the prawns on the salmon followed by the asparagus. Pour over the egg mix. Sprinkle with the reserved Parmesan. Bake for 15–20 minutes until the filling is golden and just set with a slight wobble on top.

Leave to cool before trimming off the pastry edges. Finish by snipping some fresh chives over the surface.

Cheese & ham waffles

Have I mentioned how much I love Paris? I have been lucky enough to go there several times, starting with a very interesting school exchange when I was about 12 (when I accidentally brought the Eiffel Tower to a standstill) to the past three years when Liam and I have gone every year just before Christmas. We wander, we eat, we drink red wine and we visit every market going! The inspiration for these savoury waffles comes from my last visit when, undecided about what to eat that day, I saw these being made on a stall at the start of the Champs–Élysées. We didn't stop then, but 2 hours later I wanted to go back to the stall and have a waffle. So worth the walk and soooooo tasty! This is my version – eat them straight away, while they are hot, and pretend you are in Paris!

Makes 5–10
(depending on the size of your waffle-maker)
—

250g plain flour
1 tsp baking powder
1 tsp golden caster sugar
3 eggs
100g unsalted butter, melted
400ml whole milk
1 tsp Dijon mustard
100g smoked pancetta or streaky bacon
2 spring onions, finely chopped
150g strong Cheddar or other cheese of your choice, grated
1 small bunch fresh chives, finely snipped
olive oil, for greasing
salt and freshly ground black pepper

Sift the flour and baking powder into a large bowl and mix through the sugar. Make a well in the centre and add the eggs. Whisk them together, slowly incorporating all the flour.

Mix together the melted butter and milk, then gradually pour into the bowl, whisking until all the lumps are gone and you have a nice smooth batter. Whisk in the mustard. Set aside.

Chop the pancetta or bacon into bite-sized pieces, then fry with the spring onion in a small frying pan until just cooked. Allow to cool.

Add the pancetta mixture, cheese and chives to the batter and fold in. Season well with salt and pepper.

Heat your waffle-maker. Brush it with olive oil to prevent sticking (unless it is non-stick), then add some of the batter – follow the waffle-maker instructions for the amount to use (mine uses about 240ml). Close the waffle-maker and cook for 4–5 minutes until the waffle is golden brown (turn the waffle-maker on to its other side halfway through if it is a stove-top type).

Serve immediately or place in a warm oven, covered with foil, to keep warm until the rest of the waffles are ready to serve.

Croque monsieur pancakes

Ham – yes. Cheese – yes. Mushrooms – yes. Pancakes – definitely!
These are my Croque Monsieur pancakes. Not as heavy as its bready
sister but with all the same flavour and decadence. These are perfect
for breakfast, lunch or dinner and ingredients can be added or mixed up
in whatever variation takes your fancy. Just don't scrimp on the cheese.

Serves 4
—

Parsley pancakes:
120g plain flour
2 eggs
300ml whole milk
25g unsalted butter,
   melted
1 small bunch fresh flat-
   leaf parsley, chopped

Filling:
olive oil, for frying
knob of butter
200g chestnut
   mushrooms, sliced
1 tsp chopped garlic
   (jarred or fresh)
1 tsp mushroom powder
1 tbsp chopped fresh
   parsley
200g cooked ham hock,
   shredded

Béchamel sauce:
40g unsalted butter
1 tbsp plain flour
100ml whole milk
2 tsp Dijon mustard
100g Gruyère
salt and freshly ground
   black pepper
snipped fresh chives,
   to serve

First make the batter for the pancakes. Sift the flour into a large bowl and add a pinch each of salt and pepper. Make a well in the middle and crack in the eggs. Mix together using a fork. Add the milk and mix in, whisking to remove any lumps. Add 2 tablespoons of the melted butter and whisk in. Leave to sit for about 30 minutes.

For the filling, heat a glug of olive oil with the butter in a frying pan. Add the mushrooms, garlic and mushroom powder and fry over a medium heat until the mushrooms are soft and golden. Mix in the chopped parsley and shredded ham hock. Season to taste and set aside.

Put the butter and flour for the béchamel sauce in a small saucepan and melt over a low heat, stirring. Keep stirring over the heat for 3–4 minutes. Pour in the milk a little at a time, whisking to keep the mix smooth. Keep whisking until all the milk has been added, then stir over the heat until the sauce is thick. Stir in the Dijon mustard and seasoning to taste. Remove from the heat and keep warm.

Preheat the grill to medium-high. Grease a flat, non-stick frying pan (about 12cm diameter) by wiping or brushing it with some of the remaining melted butter. Set over a medium/high heat. Ladle in enough batter to cover the bottom of the pan thinly. Fry until bubbles start to lift the pancake, then turn the pancake over (if you are feeling brave, flip or toss the pancake over). Leave for 20 seconds, then remove from the heat.

Working quite quickly, spoon some of the mushroom and ham mix over one half of the pancake, followed by some béchamel sauce and then grated cheese. Place the pan under the grill to melt the cheese. Once all the filling is bubbling, remove from the grill and fold the pancake over. Sprinkle with chives and enjoy. Make and fill the remaining pancakes in the same way.

* If you prefer, make all the pancakes,
cooking the second side for 45–60 seconds,
then arrange them in one layer on two
baking trays. Add the filling, sauce and cheese
to one half of each pancake and grill as above,
then fold over. Sprinkle with chives
and serve hot.

Tottie scones

These are actually called potato scones or 'tattie' scones but, being a bit daft, I misinterpreted the Scottish accent and they have been known to me as 'tottie' scones ever since! They are traditionally served for breakfast – I like them with eggs and bacon or, for a treat, Scottish smoked salmon and runny scrambled eggs! My Scottish other half loves them. When he was a boy he used to buy a tottie scone in a roll every day for 25p! He would never forgive me if I did not include these in my book!

Makes 6—8

—

400g peeled and chopped
   floury potatoes
100g self-raising flour,
   plus extra for dusting
large knob of butter
splash of whole milk
1 tbsp chopped fresh
   parsley
rapeseed oil, for frying
salt and freshly ground
   black pepper

Put the potatoes in a large saucepan of boiling water and cook until soft. Drain well and return to the pan (off the heat), cover with a tea towel and leave to dry out and cool down a bit.

Sift the flour into the pan and add the butter and a splash of milk. Mix until the butter has melted. Season with salt and pepper and add the parsley, then get your hands in and bring it all together.

Turn the mix out on to a lightly floured work surface and knead lightly together. Divide equally into six to eight balls. Flatten each ball with your hand to make a 4mm-thick disc about the size of a side plate. Score with a blunt knife (not cutting all the way through) in a cross from side to side.

Heat a little rapeseed oil in a frying pan over a medium heat. Place one of the scones in the pan and fry for 2–3 minutes on each side until golden brown. Transfer to a plate and keep hot while you fry the other scones.

As soon as all are fried, eat straight away (the scored cross makes it easy to break the scones into quarters). If you want to serve the tottie scones later, they can be reheated by frying for a minute on each side, or place in the toaster and lightly toast.

The title of this chapter is just begging for a Carry On innuendo!

I love the way bread goes along its own little yeast-driven journey, from a group of ingredients to a rough dough, to a smooth ball, to a giant, fat, risen and bubbly ball and then is deflated, shaped and baked into the beautiful bread we take for granted! It can be sweet or it can be savoury. It can be quick and easy or long and slow. It can be dunked in thick, hot soup or used to mop up all the delicious juices from dinner.

Nowadays an electric mixer fitted with a dough hook can take all the effort out of bread-making. But beware of over-kneading. I love kneading dough by hand. It's both therapeutic and a workout, and using your hands you'll never be able to knead too much!

Breads
& buns

Mediterranean soda bread

Soda bread is quick and easy – no resting and no kneading, and it comes out perfect every time! I'm not a fan of tomatoes, and for me sun-dried tomatoes are the worst. But according to everyone else these are essential for a Mediterranean bread. Feel free to chop and change the additions but nothing with too much water in it.

Cuts into 4 large quarters or 8 small slices

—

320ml whole milk
2 tbsp lemon juice
150g pitted black olives
100g drained sun-dried
   tomatoes
1 small bunch of fresh
   basil
300g plain flour, plus extra
   for dusting
150g strong white bread
   flour
1 tsp bicarbonate soda
½ tsp each salt and freshly
   ground black pepper
½ tsp smoked paprika
25g cold unsalted butter,
   cubed
75g Parmesan, freshly
   grated
25g mixed seeds
   (sunflower, pumpkin,
   sesame and poppy)

Preheat the oven to 180°C fan (200°C/400°F/Gas Mark 6).

Measure the milk in a measuring jug, then add the lemon juice to make up to 350ml. Stir together and set aside for a few minutes to thicken (milk and lemon = buttermilk!). Meanwhile, roughly chop the olives, sun-dried tomatoes and fresh basil.

Combine the two types of flour with the bicarbonate of soda, salt, pepper and paprika in a large bowl and mix together. Add the cubed butter and rub in with your fingertips until the mixture resembles breadcrumbs.

Add the chopped olives, sun-dried tomatoes and fresh basil, and mix with a blunt knife to incorporate evenly. Add the Parmesan and mix again with the knife.

Make a well in the mixture and add almost all the buttermilk. Mix with the blunt knife, adding more buttermilk if needed, to make a quite wet, sticky and rough dough. Finish off by getting your hands in and bringing the dough together, but do not overwork it.

Turn out the dough on to a lightly floured work surface. Shape into a large round or two smaller rounds, kneading for no more than 10–15 seconds.

Line a baking sheet with greaseproof paper and sprinkle with flour. Transfer the round(s) to the sheet. Flatten the round(s) to about 5–7.5cm thickness. With a sharp knife score a large deep cross into the top. Sprinkle with the seeds and dust with flour.

Bake a large round for 35–45 minutes, or 25–35 minutes for two smaller rounds. When done, the bread should be a deep golden colour and the cross scored on top should have opened out. To test if the bread is fully cooked, tap it on the base – it should sound hollow. Remove from the oven and place on a wire rack.

Serve warm – break off a chunk and slather it with butter – with a bowl of my Roasted Red Pepper, Squash and Sweet Potato Soup (page 184).

* The recipe calls for buttermilk, which you can buy in most supermarkets, but I always make my own from whole milk and lemon juice. It works perfectly in this soda bread.

Quick Parma ham & oregano ciabatta rolls

I think making ciabatta scares people a bit. This is a really simple version that gives great results and it's a little different with the addition of Parma ham and oregano. The dough is very wet and it is much easier to make with an electric mixer, though not impossible by hand – just messy! If you are vegetarian you can leave the Parma ham out.

Makes 4 rolls

—

250g strong white bread flour, plus extra for dusting

50g strong wholemeal flour

7g instant yeast

I tsp salt

I tsp golden caster sugar

35ml olive oil, plus extra for greasing

300ml lukewarm water

200g Parma ham, finely chopped

I tsp dried oregano

semolina, for dusting

Combine both types of flour in the large bowl of a free-standing electric mixer fitted with a dough hook and make a well in the centre. Put the yeast on one side of the well and the salt and sugar on the opposite side. Pour the olive oil and about three-quarters of the warm water into the well. Mix on a low speed, gradually drawing the flour into the liquid, for 2 minutes until the dough starts to come together.

Add the rest of the water along with the Parma ham and oregano. Turn up to medium speed and mix/knead for about 6 minutes until the dough is smooth. It will be fairly wet and very sticky.

While the dough is mixing, lightly grease a square or rectangular tub or other container with olive oil.

Tip the sticky wet dough into the greased tub, cover with a tea towel and leave to rise in a warm place for about 2 hours until the dough has at least doubled in size.

Line two baking sheets with greaseproof paper and dust with flour and semolina. Sprinkle the work surface with a mix of flour and semolina, then gently tip out the risen dough – be very gentle as you want to keep as much air in it as possible. Dust the top of the dough with more flour and semolina.

Lightly oil a sharp knife, then cut the dough in half across and then lengthways so you have four equal square/rectangular shapes. Gently lift the cut dough on to the baking sheets, placing two on each and making sure there is space in between. Again, be very gentle and try not to handle the dough too much. Allow to rest for about 15 minutes.

Preheat the oven to 200°C fan (220°C/425°F/Gas Mark 7).

Bake for 30–35 minutes until slightly risen and the top of each loaf is golden brown. If you tip a loaf off the baking sheet and tap the bottom it should sound hollow. Transfer to a wire rack to cool.

Serve warm with soup, or the next day toasted and buttered or filled with your favourite sandwich filling.

Nigella seed & onion bread

I so enjoy seeing bread do its thing. You put a few ingredients together and give it a good knead then watch it grow. I think it's amazing! The nigella seeds add a lovely little bitter onion taste against the sweet red onions but you can chop and change the seeds according to your taste. This is a great recipe to make if you've had a bad day – 10 minutes of kneading and you'll be right as rain!

Makes 2 large loaves
—

2 tsp nigella seeds
100g mixed seeds
   (sunflower, pumpkin,
   sesame and poppy)
700g strong white bread
   flour
10g fine sea salt
1 tbsp caster sugar
7g instant yeast
about 450ml lukewarm
   water
100g red onion, chopped
knob of butter

To finish:
semolina for the baking
   sheets
1 egg, beaten
2 tsp nigella seeds

Put the nigella seeds and mixed seeds in a small, dry frying pan and set over a low heat. Gently toast the seeds for a few minutes to bring out the flavour. Set aside.

Sift the flour into a large bowl. Make a well in the middle of the flour. On one side of the bowl add the salt and sugar and add the yeast to the opposite side. Add the cooled nigella seeds and mixed seeds to the well.

Slowly pour the lukewarm water into the well in the flour (do not add it all at once in case you do not need it all). Use your hand to gradually bring the flour in from the edges to mix with the water, using a circular motion. You want to make a soft, slightly sticky dough. Add more water if needed.

Turn out the dough on to a lightly floured work surface and knead for 10–12 minutes. You will see the dough change from a rough and sticky mass to a smooth and elastic dough. (You could also make the dough in a free-standing electric mixer fitted with a dough hook. Knead on the lowest speed for no longer than 5 minutes.)

Shape the dough into a ball, put it into a large, lightly oiled bowl and cover with cling film – or use a clear shower cap (the elastic will hold it firmly in place!). Leave to rise in a warm place for about 2 hours until the dough has at least doubled in size.

Meanwhile, fry the onion in the butter in a frying pan over a medium heat until softened. Allow to cool.

Using your knuckles punch the air out of the risen dough, then turn it out on to the floured work surface. Tip the cooled red onion on top of the dough and start folding the dough over on itself, kneading the onion gently through, for about 1 minute.

Continued overleaf →

Continued...

Divide the dough into two pieces and shape each into an oblong that tapers off at the ends. Cup your hands around the dough and turn and tuck the edges under as you go, so any seam will be on the underside.

Line two baking sheets with greaseproof paper and sprinkle with flour and semolina. Place a shaped loaf on each sheet. Sprinkle with flour, then cover lightly with cling film. Leave to rise in a warm, draught-free place for about 1 hour or until doubled in size.

Preheat the oven to 200°C fan (220°C/425°F/Gas Mark 7) and place a shallow roasting tin in the bottom.

Using a very sharp knife, make one or two slashes, or a cross, in the top of each loaf. Gently brush with beaten egg and sprinkle with the nigella seeds. Place in the oven. Very quickly pour a cup of water into the tin at the bottom (this creates steam), then close the oven door. Bake for 35–40 minutes – swap the baking sheets round after 20 minutes and add another cup of water to the tin in the bottom if it has dried out. To check if the loaf is cooked, tap the base – the bread should sound hollow. Transfer the loaves to a wire rack and leave to cool.

Serve with a hot baked Camembert or in toasted slices with lots of butter.

You could eat one loaf and freeze the other. As soon as it is cold, wrap up and place in the freezer.

Best bratwurst rolls

On a trip to Barcelona, Liam and I went to see Barcelona vs PSG at the Camp Nou. On the way back to the hotel we found this tiny little sausage shop owned by two old guys who had been running it for about 50 years. They only served three types of sausages in fresh bread, plus frites and one kind of beer. I know it wasn't authentic Spanish cuisine but at that moment it was perfect. This is one of our favourite meals to have at weekends and even better during the summer with the bratwursts grilled on the BBQ.

Makes 6

—

200g strong white bread flour
200g plain flour, plus extra for dusting
10g instant yeast
10g salt
1 tbsp golden caster sugar
120ml lukewarm whole milk
120ml lukewarm water
1 egg
25g unsalted butter, melted
semolina, for dusting
beaten egg, for egg wash
30g mixed seeds (pumpkin, sesame, poppy, sunflower)

Combine both types of flour in the large bowl of a free-standing electric mixer fitted with a dough hook, and make a well in the centre. Add the yeast to one side and the salt and sugar to the opposite side.

Mix the warm milk and water with the egg in a jug. Pour three-quarters of the warm mix into the well in the flour and mix on a low speed for about 2 minutes until all the flour has been incorporated.

Add the melted butter and turn the speed up to medium. If the mixture is looking too dry, add some more of the warm liquid. Mix/knead for 8–10 minutes until you have a smooth, stretchy dough.

Grease a large bowl. Transfer the dough to it and cover with cling film. Leave to rise for up to 3 hours until at least doubled in size.

Line two baking sheets with greaseproof paper and sprinkle them with semolina.

Flour a work surface, then sprinkle with semolina. Turn the risen dough out on to the surface and shape into a large rectangle about 2.5cm thick. Dust a sharp knife in flour and use to cut the dough rectangle across into six strips.

Gently pick up the strip and place on the baking sheets (three strips per sheet), leaving space in between the strips to allow for spreading. Try to give each strip a rounded sausage shape. You may need to fold them over if they have stretched. Leave to rise uncovered for about 30 minutes.

Preheat the oven to 180°C fan (200°C/400°F/Gas Mark 6).

Egg wash each roll and sprinkle with seeds. Bake for 20–25 minutes until golden brown and risen. Cool on a wire rack.

Split open and serve with bratwurst sausages, fried onions and mustard.

Saffron & cumin pikelets

These came about as I wanted to make crumpets (they were always one of mine and my brother Ben's favourite things), but I didn't have any crumpet rings (apparently using cookie cutters is not a great substitution!), so I went freestyle and made these pikelets. With the pikelet you get all the bubbly goodness of the crumpet but they are just a little thinner with a less uniform shape – which means you can have more! The cumin gives them a subtle spice flavour and the saffron makes them a gorgeous yellow colour.

Makes 12
—

200ml lukewarm milk
150ml lukewarm water
pinch of saffron threads
1 tsp cumin seeds
225g plain flour
½ tsp baking powder
1 tsp salt
1 tsp instant yeast
olive oil, for frying
salted butter, softened,
   for serving

Combine the warm milk and warm water in a measuring jug. Add the pinch of saffron and leave for a few minutes to allow the liquid to take on the gorgeous gold of the saffron.

Meanwhile, gently toast the cumin seeds in a small, dry frying pan over a low heat until fragrant. This helps to release the flavour of the cumin. Set aside.

Sift the flour and baking powder into a large bowl. To one side add the salt and to the opposite side add the yeast. Make a well in the centre of the flour and pour in three-quarters of the warm milk/water and saffron mix. Whisk together, drawing in the flour, then add the rest of the liquid and whisk well to be sure there are no lumps.

Add the cumin seeds and whisk them in. The batter should be the consistency of thick cream – pourable but thick enough to coat the back of a spoon. Cover with cling film and leave in a warm place for about 2 hours until the surface of the batter is covered in little bubbles.

Heat a glug of olive oil in a frying pan over a medium heat, then spoon in about 2 tablespoons of batter per pikelet, spacing them well apart to allow for spreading (you will need to fry them in batches). Fry for 2–3 minutes, watching as the bubbles on the surface burst to leave lots of little holes on the top before flipping and frying for 2–3 minutes on the other side. Transfer to a ovenproof plate, cover with foil and keep warm in a low oven while you fry the rest of the batter.

Serve the pikelets on a large plate, spread with salted butter, and serve immediately.

* These pikelets freeze really well. To defrost, simply toast them in the toaster until hot through.

Cumin, garlic & parsley flatbreads

Light and fluffy, with just a little bit of charring, these lovely little flatbreads are great on their own, dipped in something lovely, or as an accompaniment to chilli or curry – perfect for mopping up any sauce. If you prefer your flatbreads a little crisper then be brave and stretch them a little more. By only oiling one side you get lovely charred bits ready to be drenched in garlic butter.

Makes 5–7
—

250g strong white bread flour, plus extra for dusting
½ tsp caster sugar
5g salt
5g instant yeast
1 tsp cumin seeds
15g natural yoghurt
150ml lukewarm water
25g unsalted butter
2 tsp finely chopped garlic (jarred or fresh)
½ small bunch fresh flat-leaf parsley
olive oil

Put the flour in a large bowl. Add the sugar and salt to one side and the yeast to the opposite side. Make a well in the centre and add the cumin seeds. Tip in the yoghurt and 120ml of the water. Mix round with your hands, gathering all the flour from the edges into the liquid. Add enough of the remaining water, a little at a time, to make a soft dough.

Lightly flour a work surface and turn out the dough. Knead for 8–10 minutes until you have a smooth, stretchy dough. Shape into a ball.

Lightly grease the large bowl, then return the dough to it and cover with cling film. Leave to rise in a warm place for 1–2 hours until at least doubled in size.

Turn out the dough on to the floured surface again and fold it over on itself until all the air has been knocked out. Roll into a sausage shape and cut across into five to seven equal balls.

Using a rolling pin, roll out each ball to a round about the size of a side plate (12cm) – it doesn't matter if the rounds are a little wonky. Leave to rest for 15 minutes.

Meanwhile, melt the butter in a small saucepan and stir in the garlic and chopped parsley. Heat gently for a minute, then remove from the heat and set aside to infuse.

Heat a large frying pan or griddle on a medium/high heat. Lightly brush oil on one side of each flatbread, then fry them one at a time, oiled-side down, for 3–4 minutes. Turn over and fry for another 3–4 minutes. Remove from the pan and generously brush the garlic butter all over the hot flatbread. Keep hot in a warm oven, covered with foil, while you fry the remaining flatbreads.

Serve with my Cheesy Spinach and Artichoke Dip (see overleaf).

Cheesy spinach & artichoke dip

I eat spinach most days. I love it and feel like it makes me big and strong!
I tried something like this dip while on holiday with my family, so I made
my own version. I've given you the choice of eating it cold or baked hot
– I prefer it cold but my family like it hot. It's a great sharing dish with
flatbreads, crackers or even chips.

Serves 4–6
—

150g thawed frozen
    spinach
200g jarred artichokes
    in oil, well drained
100g Parmesan, freshly
    grated, plus extra if
    serving the dip hot
250g ricotta cheese
½ tsp onion salt
½ tsp chopped garlic
    (jarred or fresh)
salt and freshly ground
    black pepper

Squeeze out the excess water from the thawed spinach, then place in
a food processor. Ensure all the oil is drained from the artichokes, then
add to the spinach along with the grated Parmesan, ricotta, onion, salt
and garlic. Blitz until smooth. Add salt and pepper to taste.

The dip is now ready to eat or can be wrapped and kept in the fridge
for later.

You can also serve the dip hot: spoon it into an ovenproof dish, top with
extra grated Parmesan and bake in a 160°C fan (180°C/350°F/Gas Mark 4)
oven for 20 minutes until hot and slightly browned on top.

This is the perfect dip for my Nigella Seed and Onion Bread (page 217)
or my Cumin, Garlic and Parsley Flatbreads (page 223).

← *Photo on page 222*

Cointreau & orange hot cross buns

Grown-up, zesty and fruity hot cross buns, traditional yet modern. The saffron makes these buns a beautiful soft yellow colour and the subtle flavour complements the tangy orange zest and cranberries soaked plump in orange liqueur. The buns are best served warm, spread with butter, or toasted the next day.

Makes 8
—

100ml whole milk
½ cinnamon stick, broken
pinch of saffron threads
seeds from 3 cardamom
   pods, lightly crushed
7g instant yeast
25g golden caster sugar
250g strong white bread
   flour, plus extra for
   dusting
¼ tsp ground cinnamon
¼ tsp freshly grated
   nutmeg
50g unsalted butter
7g salt
1 egg
50g sultanas
25g dried cranberries
25g mixed candied peel
grated zest of 1 orange
100ml Cointreau

To finish:
2 tbsp plain flour
beaten egg, for egg wash
1 tbsp golden caster sugar
25ml boiling water

Put the milk, cinnamon stick, saffron and cardamom seeds in a small saucepan and slowly bring to the boil. Remove from the heat and cool to lukewarm.

Strain the now fragrant milk into a small bowl and add the yeast and 1½ tablespoons of the sugar. Stir to mix.

Sift the bread flour, ground cinnamon and nutmeg into the large bowl of a free-standing electric mixer fitted with a dough hook. Add the butter and rub in until the mixture resembles breadcrumbs. Add the salt and remaining sugar. Make a well in the centre.

Pour the warm milk and yeast mix into the well and add the egg. Mix on a low speed for 2 minutes until the dough comes together, then mix/knead on medium speed for 5–6 minutes until you have a soft, smooth, elastic dough.

Turn out the dough on to a floured work surface and gently smooth into a ball. Place in a lightly greased bowl, cover with cling film and leave to rise for about 2 hours until at least doubled in size.

Combine the sultanas, cranberries and mixed peel in a small bowl and add the orange zest and Cointreau. Mix, then leave the fruit to absorb the orange liqueur.

Once the dough has risen, turn it out on to a lightly floured surface and knock the air out. Flatten the dough slightly. Scoop out the now plumped dried fruit (try to drain off as much liquid as possible; keep this liquid) and place on top of the dough. Sprinkle with a little flour, then knead together until the fruit is evenly incorporated.

Divide into eight pieces and roll each into a ball. Place on a baking sheet lined with greaseproof paper, leaving space around each ball. Put the sheet into a clean plastic bag and leave in a warm place for 45–60 minutes until risen and springy to the touch.

Preheat the oven to 180°C fan (200°C/400°F/Gas Mark 6).

In a small bowl, stir the plain flour with enough of the dried fruit soaking liquid to make a smooth paste. Put into a small piping bag and snip a small hole in the end.

Once the buns have risen, egg wash them, then pipe a cross on top of each bun using the flour paste. Bake for 20–25 minutes until the buns are golden brown.

Meanwhile, dissolve 1 tablespoon sugar in the boiling water. As soon as the hot cross buns come out of the oven, brush them with this sugar glaze. Cool on a wire rack.

Serve split and toasted with lashings of butter melting on top.

!! If you're making these for children, swap the Cointreau for orange juice. You could also use chocolate chunks rather than dried fruit.

Photo overleaf →

Apple, walnut & cinnamon buns

Hot sticky breakfast bun, anyone? Yes please! These are best eaten warm from the oven, with your hands, so prepare to get sticky. The buns are indulgent and super-sweet, with a hint of spice. The addition of apple creates a gorgeous syrup as the buns rise, which adds to the sweet stickiness! Trust me on this, one will not be enough.

Makes 10
—

Dough:
500g strong white bread
   flour, plus extra for
   dusting
1 tsp salt
2 tsp golden caster sugar
275ml whole milk
50g unsalted butter
1 tsp ground cinnamon
7g instant yeast
1 egg

Filling:
100g unsalted butter,
   softened
200g light soft brown
   sugar
3 tsp ground cinnamon
3 crisp eating apples,
   peeled, cored and diced
100g walnuts, chopped
25g demerara sugar
½ tsp freshly grated
   nutmeg
150ml good-quality maple
   syrup

Sift the flour into the large bowl of an electric mixer fitted with a dough hook. Mix through the salt and sugar.

In a small saucepan gently warm the milk with the butter and cinnamon until the butter has melted and the mix is lukewarm.

Make a well in the flour. Add the yeast to the well, then pour in the warm milk followed by the egg. Mix on a low speed for 4–5 minutes until you have a smooth, stretchy dough. (You can also make the dough by hand but you will need to knead for 9–10 minutes.)

Shape the dough into a ball, then put it into a lightly greased large bowl and cover with cling film. Leave to rise in a warm place for about 1½ hours until at least doubled in size.

Turn out the dough on to a lightly floured work surface and fold it over on itself until all the air has been knocked out. Roll out the dough to a 25 x 45cm rectangle.

In a bowl mash together the softened butter, sugar and cinnamon. Stir through the diced apples and chopped walnuts. Spread this evenly over the rolled-out dough.

Taking one of the long edges, start to roll up the dough tightly. Make sure the first roll is tucked under. When it is all rolled up, gently roll the whole thing back and forth to seal the join. Using a sharp knife or dough cutter, cut the rolled-up dough across into 10 equal pieces about 3–4cm wide.

Line a 25cm square tin or a 25cm round deep tin with greaseproof paper. Place the dough pieces in the lined tin, setting them on a cut side (swirl side up) and leaving about a 1cm gap around each one.

Sprinkle with the demerara sugar and nutmeg. Place the tin in a clean plastic bag and leave in a warm place for about 30 minutes until risen. The apple and sugar will create a gorgeous juice in the bottom of the tin, which will be absorbed by the buns as they bake.

Preheat the oven to 160°C fan (180°C/350°F/Gas Mark 4).

Bake the buns for 20–30 minutes (cover with foil if they are browning too quickly).

Remove from the oven and drench the buns in maple syrup. Allow to cool for 10 minutes, then turn the buns over in the tin so they get completely covered in syrup. Pull apart the buns and serve warm.

*When adding the filling to the dough, lightly greasing the work surface with some olive oil, instead of dusting it with more flour, avoids the dough getting too dry.

You could also
make two smaller
plaits. Just divide the
dough in half at step
6 and bake for
25–30 minutes.

Ginger & chocolate plait

It's safe to say I have had a love/hate relationship with chocolate bread but this, rich in chocolate and cinnamon, with the fieriness of ginger, has restored my faith in chocolate loveliness in all its plaited splendour. My Grandad loved crystallised ginger and we used to laugh as he'd roll a piece around his mouth, pulling faces as the heat set in. He would've loved this bread.

Serves 10

—

500g strong white bread
   flour, plus extra for
   dusting
1 tsp salt
2 tsp golden caster sugar
275ml whole milk
50g unsalted butter
1 tsp ground ginger
7g instant yeast
1 egg

Filling:

100g unsalted butter,
   softened
100g light soft brown
   sugar
1 tsp ground ginger
½ tsp ground cinnamon
75g dark chocolate
   (minimum 70% cocoa
   solids), finely chopped
75g chopped crystallised
   stem ginger
25g unsalted butter,
   melted
20g demerara sugar

Sift the flour into the large bowl of a free-standing electric mixer fitted with a dough hook. Mix through the salt and sugar.

In a small saucepan gently warm the milk with the butter and ginger until the butter has melted and the mix is lukewarm.

Make a well in the flour. Add the yeast to the well, then pour in the warm milk followed by the egg. Mix on a low speed for 4–5 minutes until you have a smooth, stretchy dough. (Alternatively, make the dough by hand and knead it for 9–10 minutes.)

Shape the dough into a ball, then put it into a lightly greased large bowl and cover with cling film. Leave to rise in a warm place for about 1½ hours until at least doubled in size.

Turn out the dough on to a lightly floured work surface and fold it over on itself to knock out the air. Roll out the dough to a 25 x 45cm rectangle.

Mash the softened butter, brown sugar, ginger and cinnamon in a bowl. Spread this evenly over the dough. Scatter the chopped chocolate and ginger evenly over the top.

Taking one of the long edges, start to roll up the dough tightly. Make sure the first roll is tucked under. Now use a rolling pin to roll out the dough to a rectangle about 10 x 45cm. Be gentle to prevent breaking the dough. Cut the dough lengthways into three equal strips, leaving a 2cm section at one end intact so the strips are joined there. Starting at the joined end, plait the three strips together, keeping the plait tight and trying not to let the open sides turn out. Squeeze the ends together and tuck them under the plait. Brush the plait with the melted butter and sprinkle on the demerara sugar.

Line a baking sheet with greaseproof paper and lightly dust with flour. Gently lift the plait on to the sheet. Cover lightly with a tea towel and leave to rise for about 30 minutes.

Preheat the oven to 160°C fan (180°C/350°F/Gas Mark 4).

Bake the plait for 45–60 minutes until it is golden brown and risen; if you tip it over and tap the base it should sound hollow.

* Don't overfill the dough
or you will lose the definition
of the strands. If this does
happen though, don't panic:
an overfilled plait will
work well as a couronne
or as individual rolls.
Either way, they won't be
around for long!

Rhubarb syllabub doughnuts

You can't eat a whole one of these without licking your lips – a classic pudding rejigged in doughnut form. Tart rhubarb cooked in white wine and sugar teamed with sweet vanilla cream, both piped into soft, plump balls of deep-fried dough. What's not to like? These are pretty big doughnuts, so if you can't handle the size then you are better off making 12 smaller ones. (I know you will still eat two though!)

Makes 6 large or 12 small doughnuts
—

Dough:
270g strong white bread flour, plus extra for dusting
10g instant yeast
10g salt
20g caster sugar, plus optional extra for dredging
finely grated zest of 1 lemon
120ml lukewarm whole milk
40g unsalted butter, very soft
1 egg
rapeseed oil

Put the flour in the large bowl of a free-standing electric mixer fitted with a dough hook. Make a small well in the middle. To one side put the yeast and on the opposite side put the salt, sugar and lemon zest. Pour the lukewarm milk, the very soft butter and egg into the well.

Mix on a low speed for 2 minutes until everything is combined. Turn up the speed slightly and mix/knead for 5 minutes until you have a smooth, soft dough. (You can also make the dough by hand, kneading on a lightly oiled surface for 10 minutes.)

Turn out the dough on to a lightly oiled work surface and shape into a smooth ball. Place in a lightly greased large bowl and cover with a clean tea towel. Leave to rise in a warm place for 1–2 hours until at least doubled in size.

Turn out the risen dough on to a lightly floured surface. Slightly knock out the air, then divide equally into either six large balls or 12 mini balls. Gently pinch and pull the outside of each ball into the middle so you get a nice smooth, round shape. Arrange the balls, not touching each other, on a baking sheet lined with greaseproof paper. Place this in a clean plastic bag and leave for 45–60 minutes until doubled in size.

Heat 10–15cm of rapeseed oil in a high-sided medium-sized saucepan or deep-fat fryer until the oil reaches 150°C (302°F). Deep-fry the doughnuts in batches – no more than three at a time – and check the oil temperature between each batch. Carefully place the dough balls into the oil. If they are large, fry for 3 minutes on each side; fry small balls for 2 minutes on each side. When done, the doughnuts will be puffed and golden brown. Lift out with a slotted spoon and place on kitchen paper to drain.

Filling:
200g fresh rhubarb,
   chopped into small
   pieces
2 tbsp medium/sweet
   white wine
1 tbsp golden caster sugar
grated zest of 1 orange
150ml double cream
150g mascarpone cheese
1 tbsp icing sugar
½ tsp vanilla bean paste

To finish (optional):
100g icing sugar, sifted

At this point you can roll the warm doughnuts in caster sugar if you like.

Put the rhubarb, white wine, golden caster sugar and orange zest in a small saucepan. Set on a low/medium heat and cook until the rhubarb is softened and the liquid has reduced to a thick syrup. Transfer 1 tablespoon of the syrup to a small bowl. Set the pan of rhubarb aside to cool.

In another bowl, combine the double cream, mascarpone, icing sugar and vanilla and whisk together until the mix is just thickened and will hold its shape. Spoon the cream mixture into a piping bag fitted with a fairly large round nozzle. Fill a second piping bag fitted with a fairly large, round nozzle with the rhubarb mix.

Using a chopstick, poke two holes side by side into the side of each doughnut – give the chopstick a wiggle around so you create space inside the doughnut. Pipe the cream mix into one hole and the rhubarb mix into the other hole (be careful as this mix is a little thinner and may run).

If you haven't rolled the doughnuts in caster sugar, then make a glaze with the reserved rhubarb syrup and the icing sugar. Drizzle this over the top of the filled doughnuts.

* No white wine to hand? Try using a sweet vermouth with the rhubarb instead.

Photo overleaf →

Spiced sultana bagels

I love the process of making bagels – boiling dough might seem a little strange but it's completely essential if you want your bagels to have that shiny crust and trademark chewiness! Even though bagels are essentially a sweet bread rich with sultanas and spice, they still taste amazing toasted, buttered and grilled with melted cheese on top. It works, trust me! My absolute favourite topping is heaps of peanut butter.

Makes 6

—

225g strong white bread flour, plus extra for dusting

1 tsp salt

1 tbsp light soft brown sugar, plus 2 tsp for boiling

½ tsp ground cinnamon

½ tsp ground ginger

finely grated zest of 1 lemon

75g sultanas

1 tsp instant yeast

150ml lukewarm water

beaten egg, for egg wash

Sift the flour into a large bowl and make a well in the centre. To one side add the salt, 1 tablespoon sugar, cinnamon and ginger, then sprinkle over the lemon zest and sultanas. To the opposite side add the yeast.

Pour three-quarters of the water into the well and mix round in circles with your hand, gradually bringing the flour in from the edge. Add the rest of the water and bring together to form a dough that leaves the side of the bowl clean.

Tip out the dough on to a lightly floured work surface and knead for about 8 minutes until you have a smooth dough that will hold its shape.

Lightly grease the bowl, then put the dough back into it. Cover with cling film and leave to rise in a warm place for about 2 hours until at least doubled in size.

Turn out the risen dough on to the floured surface again and knock the air out by pushing your knuckles into the dough three times, then kneading lightly for 2 minutes. Roll the dough into a sausage shape and cut across into six equal-sized pieces. Roll each piece into a smooth ball, pinching the edges and pulling them into the middle.

Line a baking sheet with greaseproof paper. Dust a finger with flour, then poke it into a ball, wiggling your finger around a few times to stretch the hole size and shape a ring. Place the ring of dough on the lined baking sheet. Shape the other pieces and set them on the sheet, spaced well apart to allow for spreading. Put the baking sheet inside a clean plastic bag and leave in a warm place for about 30 minutes until the rings are risen and springy to the touch.

Preheat the oven to 180°C fan (200°C/400°F/Gas Mark 6). Put a large saucepan of water on a medium/high heat and bring to the boil.

Once the water is boiling, add the 2 teaspoons brown sugar, then gently lower two of the bagel rings into the boiling water. Boil for 45 seconds before carefully flipping over and boiling for 45 seconds on the other side. Using a slotted spoon, remove the bagel rings from the water, draining well, and return to the lined tray. Repeat with the remaining bagel rings.

Brush the bagel rings with the egg wash, then bake for about 20 minutes until risen and golden. Transfer to a wire rack to cool. Serve warm on their own or split and toast lightly before spreading with a thick helping of crunchy peanut butter.

* These bagels are best eaten on the day they are baked. For longer storage, freeze them, then thaw and lightly toast.

Index

A

ale: beef & ale pies, mash & liquor 186–7

almonds

almond & pear pinwheel pastries 104–5

back-to-front chocolate & pear profiteroles 100–1

berry crème tarts 98

Black Forest gateau 46–7

cherry Amaretto Bakewell tart 93

granola 84

hidden clove, apple & strawberry strudel 139–40

lime & kiwi cheesecake 145

marzipan 52–3

marzipan mince pies 109

mint chocolate cake 34

Nan's florentines 69

port-soaked Christmas cake 52–3

raspberry & custard almond cake 50

Amaretto

berry crème tarts 98

cherry Amaretto Bakewell tart 93

apples

apple & pear crumble muffins 61

apple, walnut & cinnamon buns 230–1

apricot, apple & cashew flapjacks 74

bramble apple pie 137

hidden clove, apple & strawberry strudel 139–40

marzipan mince pies 109

pork & apple pasties 164

toffee apple crumble 120

apricots

apricot, apple & cashew flapjacks 74

Nan's boiled fruit cake 41

Nan's florentines 69

port-soaked Christmas cake 52–3

artichokes: cheesy spinach & artichoke dip 224

asparagus: salmon, prawn & asparagus tart 204

B

back-to-front chocolate & pear profiteroles 100–1

bacon

black pudding sausage rolls 167–8

cheese & ham waffles 207

chicken stew with pesto & pine nut dumplings 182–3

choose-your-lid chicken pie 196–7

decadent cauliflower cheese 177

macaroni pies 199–200

pork & apple pasties 164

bagels, spiced sultana 240–1

Bakewell tart, cherry Amaretto 93

bananas

carrot cake 38–9

chocolate & banana waffles 146

coconut, banana and dark chocolate loaf 57

individual banoffee pies 135–6

basil: Mediterranean soda bread 214

béchamel sauce: croque monsieur pancakes 208

beef & ale pies, mash & liquor 186–7

berries

berry crème tarts 98

jam jam jam 152

triple-layer berry Victoria sponge 31–2

biscotti, cranberry, orange & hazelnut 75

biscuits

chewy chocolate orange cookies 77

cranberry, orange & hazelnut biscotti 75

macadamia nut & raspberry jam biscuits 78–9

millionaire shortbread hearts 83

Black Forest gateau 46–7

black pudding sausage rolls 167–8

blackberries

bramble apple pie 137

gooseberry fool éclairs 116–17

lemon & blackberry drizzle loaf 44

blondies, peanut butter & marshmallow 66

blueberries: berry crème tarts 98

bramble apple pie 137

bratwurst rolls, best 220

brazil nuts: port-soaked Christmas cake 52–3

bread

best bratwurst rolls 220

bread sauce 172–3

cumin, garlic & parsley flatbreads 223

ginger & chocolate plait 233

marmalade, cardamom & chocolate bread & butter pudding 124

Mediterranean soda bread 214

nigella seed & onion bread 217–18

quick Parma ham & oregano ciabatta rolls 216

breadcrumbs
    decadent cauliflower cheese 177
    ham hock & chorizo Scotch eggs 171
brittle, pecan 38–9
brownies
    chocolate hazelnut brownies 73
    Nan's butterscotch brownies 68
    peanut butter & marshmallow blondies 66
buns
    apple, walnut & cinnamon buns 230–1
    Cointreau & orange hot cross buns 226–7
buttercream 58
butternut squash
    chicken stew with pesto & pine nut dumplings 182–3
    roasted red pepper, squash & sweet potato soup 184
butterscotch: Nan's butterscotch brownies 68

C
cakes
    apple & pear crumble muffins 61
    carrot cake 38–9
    chocolate hazelnut brownies 73
    coconut, banana and dark chocolate loaf 57
    date & ginger cake 37
    hidden cherry & lemon cupcakes 58
    lemon & blackberry drizzle loaf 44
    lemon, gin & poppy seed cake 40
    mint chocolate cake 34
    mocha chocolate cake 30
    Nan's boiled fruit cake 41
    Nan's butterscotch brownies 68
    orange & hibiscus madeleines 62
    peanut butter & marshmallow blondies 66
    port-soaked Christmas cake 52–3
    raspberry & custard almond cake 50
    rhubarb & custard ring 54
Cambozola: decadent cauliflower cheese 177
Cape gooseberries: gooseberry fool éclairs 116–17
caramel
    individual banoffee pies 135–6
    Ivy's Malteser ice cream 148
    millionaire shortbread hearts 83
cardamom
    chewy chocolate orange cookies 77
    marmalade, cardamom & chocolate bread & butter
        pudding 124

carrots
    beef & ale pies, mash & liquor 186–7
    carrot cake 38–9
    chicken stew with pesto & pine nut dumplings 182–3
    chunky shepherd's pie 191–2
    leftover chicken & everything soup 181
    swede and carrot mash with cumin 172–3
cashews: apricot, apple & cashew flapjacks 74
cauliflower cheese, decadent 177
cheese
    cheese & ham waffles 207
    cheese & mushroom Danish rounds 108
    cheese & onion pie 202–3
    cheesy spinach & artichoke dip 224
    chorizo, pepper & sweet potato tart 195
    chunky shepherd's pie 191–2
    croque monsieur pancakes 208
    decadent cauliflower cheese 177
    fish pie 198
    macaroni pies 199–200
    Mediterranean soda bread 214
    pesto & pine nut dumplings 182–3
    salmon, prawn & asparagus tart 204
    Stilton twisted straws 158–9
    vegetable quiche 190
cheesecake, lime & kiwi 145
cherries
    Black Forest gateau 46–7
    cherry Amaretto Bakewell tart 93
    hidden cherry & lemon cupcakes 58
    Nan's boiled fruit cake 41
    Nan's florentines 69
    port-soaked Christmas cake 52–3
chewy chocolate orange cookies 77
chicken
    chicken stew with pesto & pine nut dumplings 182–3
    choose-your-lid chicken pie 196–7
    family roast chicken with all the trimmings 172–3
    leftover chicken & everything soup 181
chocolate
    back-to-front chocolate & pear profiteroles 100–1
    Black Forest gateau 46–7
    chewy chocolate orange cookies 77
    chocolate & banana waffles 146
    chocolate ganache 46–7
    chocolate hazelnut brownies 73
    coconut, banana and dark chocolate loaf 57

coconut layers 86
cranberry, orange & hazelnut biscotti 75
ginger & chocolate plait 233
gooseberry fool éclairs 116–17
individual banoffee pies 135–6
Ivy's Malteser ice cream 148
marmalade, cardamom & chocolate bread & butter
 pudding 124
millionaire shortbread hearts 83
mint chocolate cake 34
mocha chocolate cake 30
mocha ganache 30
Nan's butterscotch brownies 68
Nan's florentines 69
peanut butter & marshmallow blondies 66
piña colada macaroons 87
3 P's roulade 141
choose-your-lid chicken pie 196–7
chorizo
chorizo, pepper & sweet potato tart 195
chunky shepherd's pie 191–2
ham hock & chorizo Scotch eggs 171
choux pastry
back-to-front chocolate & pear profiteroles 100–1
gooseberry fool éclairs 116–17
Christmas cake, port-soaked 52–3
chunky shepherd's pie 191–2
chutney, sticky red onion 154
ciabatta rolls, quick Parma ham & oregano 216
cider
choose-your-lid chicken pie 196–7
pork & apple pasties 164
cinnamon: apple, walnut & cinnamon buns 230–1
cloves: hidden clove, apple & strawberry strudel 139–40
coconut
carrot cake 38–9
coconut, banana and dark chocolate loaf 57
coconut layers 86
cornflake tart 97
granola 84
Nan's florentines 69
piña colada macaroons 87
coffee
mocha chocolate cake 30
mocha ganache 30
Cointreau & orange hot cross buns 226–7
condensed milk: piña colada macaroons 87

cookies, chewy chocolate orange 77
cornflake tart 97
coulis, raspberry 113–14
courgettes
mocha chocolate cake 30
vegetable quiche 190
cranberries
Cointreau & orange hot cross buns 226–7
cranberry, orange & hazelnut biscotti 75
Nan's boiled fruit cake 41
port-soaked Christmas cake 52–3
cream
back-to-front chocolate & pear profiteroles 100–1
Black Forest gateau 46–7
coconut layers 86
fish pie 198
gooseberry fool éclairs 116–17
individual banoffee pies 135–6
Ivy's Malteser ice cream 148
lime & kiwi cheesecake 145
mango & raspberry Pavlova 127–8
marmalade, cardamom & chocolate bread & butter
 pudding 124
red, white & blue meringues 130–1
3 P's roulade 141
triple-layer berry Victoria sponge 31–2
vanilla custard 121
crème fraîche: choose-your-lid chicken pie 196–7
crème pâtissière: berry crème tarts 98
croissants 94–5
croque monsieur pancakes 208
crumble
apple & pear crumble muffins 61
plum, nectarine & ginger crumble 123
toffee apple crumble 120
cumin
cumin, garlic & parsley flatbreads 223
saffron & cumin pikelets 221
swede and carrot mash with cumin 172–3
cupcakes
apple & pear crumble muffins 61
hidden cherry & lemon cupcakes 58
curds
mango curd 154
passion fruit curd 155
custard
apple & pear crumble muffins 61

raspberry & custard almond cake 50
rhubarb & custard ring 54
vanilla custard 121

D

Danish pastries
almond & pear pinwheel pastries 104–5
cheese & mushroom Danish rounds 108
dates
date & ginger cake 37
granola 84
port-soaked Christmas cake 52–3
sticky toffee pudding 126
toffee apple crumble 120
decadent cauliflower cheese 177
dip, cheesy spinach & artichoke 224
doughnuts, rhubarb syllabub 236–7
dried fruit
Nan's boiled fruit cake 41
port-soaked Christmas cake 52–3
drizzle loaf, lemon & blackberry 44
dumplings, chicken stew with pesto & pine nut 182–3

E

éclairs, gooseberry fool 116–17
eggs
fish pie 198
ham hock & chorizo Scotch eggs 171
Ivy's Malteser ice cream 148
mango & raspberry Pavlova 127–8
mango curd 154
passion fruit curd 155
peach melba meringue pie 113–14
red, white & blue meringues 130–1
elderflower: red grapefruit & elderflower sorbet 149
evaporated milk: Nan's butterscotch brownies 68

F

family roast chicken with all the trimmings 172–3
fennel seeds: pork scratchings 162
feta cheese: vegetable quiche 190
figs: pear & fig tarte tatin 110–11
filo pastry: individual banoffee pies 135–6
fish
fish pie 198
salmon, prawn & asparagus tart 204
flapjacks, apricot, apple & cashew 74

flatbreads, cumin, garlic & parsley 223
florentines, Nan's 69
frosting, soft cheese 38–9
fruit
jam jam jam 152
see also apples; bananas, etc
fruit cakes
Nan's boiled fruit cake 41
port-soaked Christmas cake 52–3

G

ganache
chocolate ganache 46–7
mocha ganache 30
garlic: cumin, garlic & parsley flatbreads 223
gateau, Black Forest 46–7
gin: lemon, gin & poppy seed cake 40
ginger
date & ginger cake 37
ginger & chocolate plait 233
plum, nectarine & ginger crumble 123
ginger beer: date & ginger cake 37
glacé cherries: Nan's boiled fruit cake 41
golden syrup
Black Forest gateau 46–7
cornflake tart 97
date & ginger cake 37
gooseberry fool éclairs 116–17
granola 84
chocolate & banana waffles 146
plum, nectarine & ginger crumble 123
grapefruit: red grapefruit & elderflower sorbet 149
gravy 172–3
Gruyère cheese
croque monsieur pancakes 208
salmon, prawn & asparagus tart 204

H

ham
cheese & ham waffles 207
croque monsieur pancakes 208
ham hock & chorizo Scotch eggs 171
quick Parma ham & oregano ciabatta rolls 216
hazelnuts
chocolate hazelnut brownies 73
cranberry, orange & hazelnut biscotti 75
granola 84

hibiscus petals: orange & hibiscus madeleines 62
hidden cherry & lemon cupcakes 58
hidden clove, apple & strawberry strudel 139–40
hot cross buns, Cointreau & orange 226–7

I
ice cream, Ivy's Malteser 148
icing, royal 52–3
Italian meringue: peach melba meringue pie 113–14
Ivy's Malteser ice cream 148

J
jam
  cherry Amaretto jam 93
  jam jam jam 152
  raspberry jam 78–9

K
Kirsch: Black Forest gateau 46–7
kiwi fruits: lime & kiwi cheesecake 145

L
lamb: chunky shepherd's pie 191–2
leeks
  beef & ale pies, mash & liquor 186–7
  chicken stew with pesto & pine nut dumplings 182–3
  choose-your-lid chicken pie 196–7
  chunky shepherd's pie 191–2
  decadent cauliflower cheese 177
  family roast chicken with all the trimmings 172–3
  leftover chicken & everything soup 181
  pork & apple pasties 164
leftover chicken & everything soup 181
lemon thyme: lemon & blackberry drizzle loaf 44
lemons
  hidden cherry & lemon cupcakes 58
  lemon & blackberry drizzle loaf 44
  lemon, gin & poppy seed cake 40
limes
  lime & kiwi cheesecake 145
  mango curd 154
liquor 186–7
loaf cakes
  coconut, banana and dark chocolate loaf 57
  lemon & blackberry drizzle loaf 44

M
macadamia nut & raspberry jam biscuits 78–9
macaroni pies 199–200
macaroons, piña colada 87
madeleines, orange & hibiscus 62
Maltesers: Ivy's Malteser ice cream 148
Manchego cheese: chorizo, pepper & sweet potato tart 195
mangoes
  mango & raspberry Pavlova 127–8
  mango curd 154
maple syrup
  apple, walnut & cinnamon buns 230–1
  granola 84
marmalade, cardamom & chocolate bread & butter pudding 124
marshmallows: peanut butter & marshmallow blondies 66
marzipan 52–3
  marzipan mince pies 109
  port-soaked Christmas cake 52–3
mascarpone
  mango & raspberry Pavlova 127–8
  rhubarb syllabub doughnuts 236–7
Mediterranean soda bread 214
meringues
  mango & raspberry Pavlova 127–8
  peach melba meringue pie 113–14
  red, white & blue meringues 130–1
millionaire shortbread hearts 83
mince pies, marzipan 109
mint chocolate cake 34
mixed candied peel
  Cointreau & orange hot cross buns 226–7
  Nan's boiled fruit cake 41
  port-soaked Christmas cake 52–3
mocha chocolate cake 30
mozzarella
  fish pie 198
  pesto & pine nut dumplings 182–3
muffins, apple & pear crumble 61
mushrooms
  beef & ale pies, mash & liquor 186–7
  black pudding sausage rolls 167–8
  cheese & mushroom Danish rounds 108
  chicken stew with pesto & pine nut dumplings 182–3
  choose-your-lid chicken pie 196–7

chunky shepherd's pie 191–2
croque monsieur pancakes 208
leftover chicken & everything soup 181
vegetable quiche 190

N
Nan's boiled fruit cake 41
Nan's butterscotch brownies 68
Nan's florentines 69
nectarines: plum, nectarine & ginger crumble 123
nigella seed & onion bread 217–18

O
oats
apple & pear crumble muffins 61
apricot, apple & cashew flapjacks 74
granola 84
plum, nectarine & ginger crumble 123
toffee apple crumble 120
olives: Mediterranean soda bread 214
one-cup sage and onion Yorkshire puddings 178
onions
cheese & onion pie 202–3
nigella seed & onion bread 217–18
one-cup sage and onion Yorkshire puddings 178
sticky red onion chutney 154
venison sausage & red onion toad in the hole 163
oranges
chewy chocolate orange cookies 77
Cointreau & orange hot cross buns 226–7
cranberry, orange & hazelnut biscotti 75
orange & hibiscus madeleines 62
oregano: quick Parma ham & oregano ciabatta rolls 216

P
pancakes, croque monsieur 208
pancetta: cheese & ham waffles 207
Parma ham: quick Parma ham & oregano ciabatta
rolls 216
Parmesan
cheesy spinach & artichoke dip 224
Mediterranean soda bread 214
salmon, prawn & asparagus tart 204
parsley
croque monsieur pancakes 208
cumin, garlic & parsley flatbreads 223

passion fruit
mango & raspberry Pavlova 127–8
passion fruit curd 155
3 P's roulade 141
pasta: macaroni pies 199–200
pasties, pork & apple 164
pastries
almond & pear pinwheel pastries 104–5
cheese & mushroom Danish rounds 108
croissants 94–5
Stilton twisted straws 158–9
pâte sucrée
cherry Amaretto Bakewell tart 93
peach melba meringue pie 113–14
Pavlova, mango & raspberry 127–8
peach melba meringue pie 113–14
peanut butter
chocolate hazelnut brownies 73
peanut butter & marshmallow blondies 66
pearl barley: leftover chicken & everything soup 181
pears
almond & pear pinwheel pastries 104–5
apple & pear crumble muffins 61
back-to-front chocolate & pear profiteroles 100–1
pear & fig tarte tatin 110–11
pecan nuts
carrot cake 38–9
Nan's florentines 69
pear & fig tarte tatin 110–11
pecan brittle 38–9
sticky toffee pudding 126
toffee apple crumble 120
peppers
beef & ale pies, mash & liquor 186–7
chicken stew with pesto & pine nut dumplings 182–3
chorizo, pepper & sweet potato tart 195
chunky shepherd's pie 191–2
roasted red pepper, squash & sweet potato soup 184
vegetable quiche 190
pesto: chicken stew with pesto & pine nut dumplings
182–3
physalis: gooseberry fool éclairs 116–17
pies
beef & ale pies, mash & liquor 186–7
bramble apple pie 137
cheese & onion pie 202–3
choose-your-lid chicken pie 196–7

fish pie 198
individual banoffee pies 135–6
macaroni pies 199–200
marzipan mince pies 109
peach melba meringue pie 113–14
pikelets, saffron & cumin 221
piña colada macaroons 87
pine nuts: chicken stew with pesto & pine nut
   dumplings 182–3
pineapple
   carrot cake 38–9
   piña colada macaroons 87
pinwheel pastries, almond & pear 104–5
pistachios: 3 P's roulade 141
plum, nectarine & ginger crumble 123
pollock: fish pie 198
pomegranate: 3 P's roulade 141
poppy seeds
   lemon, gin & poppy seed cake 40
   Stilton twisted straws 158–9
pork
   black pudding sausage rolls 167–8
   pork & apple pasties 164
   pork scratchings 162
port-soaked Christmas cake 52–3
potatoes
   beef & ale pies, mash & liquor 186–7
   cheese & onion pie 202–3
   chunky shepherd's pie 191–2
   fish pie 198
   pork & apple pasties 164
   roast potatoes 172–3
   tottie scones 211
prawns
   fish pie 198
   salmon, prawn & asparagus tart 204
profiteroles, back-to-front chocolate & pear 100–1
puddings: toffee apple crumble 120
pumpkin seeds: spring greens 172–3

Q
quiche, vegetable 190

R
raisins
   Nan's boiled fruit cake 41
   port-soaked Christmas cake 52–3

raspberries
   macadamia nut & raspberry jam biscuits 78–9
   mango & raspberry Pavlova 127–8
   peach melba meringue pie 113–14
   raspberry & custard almond cake 50
   triple-layer berry Victoria sponge 31–2
raspberry jam: cornflake tart 97
redcurrants: berry crème tarts 98
rhubarb
   poached rhubarb 54
   rhubarb & custard ring 54
   rhubarb syllabub doughnuts 236–7
ricotta cheese
   cheesy spinach & artichoke dip 224
   fish pie 198
rolls
   best bratwurst rolls 220
   quick Parma ham & oregano ciabatta rolls 216
rosemary: venison sausage & red onion toad in
   the hole 163
roulade, 3 P's 141
royal icing 52–3

S
saffron & cumin pikelets 221
sage: one-cup sage and onion Yorkshire puddings 178
salmon
   fish pie 198
   salmon, prawn & asparagus tart 204
salted caramel 135–6
   Ivy's Malteser ice cream 148
satsumas: marzipan mince pies 109
sauce, bread 172–3
sausage rolls, black pudding 167–8
sausages: venison sausage & red onion toad in
   the hole 163
Scotch eggs, ham hock & chorizo 171
scratchings, pork 162
seeds
   best bratwurst rolls 220
   granola 84
   ham hock & chorizo Scotch eggs 171
   Mediterranean soda bread 214
   nigella seed & onion bread 217–18
   Stilton twisted straws 158–9
sesame seeds
   spring greens 172–3

Stilton twisted straws 158–9
shepherd's pie, chunky 191–2
shortbread
  macadamia nut & raspberry jam biscuits 78–9
  millionaire shortbread hearts 83
shortcrust pastry
  bramble apple pie 137
  marzipan mince pies 109
smoked haddock: fish pie 198
soda bread, Mediterranean 214
soft cheese
  coconut layers 86
  lime & kiwi cheesecake 145
  soft cheese frosting 38–9
sorbet, red grapefruit & elderflower 149
soups
  leftover chicken & everything soup 181
  roasted red pepper, squash & sweet potato soup 184
  spiced sultana bagels 240–1
spinach
  cheesy spinach & artichoke dip 224
  fish pie 198
  leftover chicken & everything soup 181
spring greens: family roast chicken with all the
  trimmings 172–3
squash
  chicken stew 182–3
  roasted red pepper, squash & sweet potato soup 184
stew: chicken stew with pesto & pine nut
  dumplings 182–3
sticky red onion chutney 154
sticky toffee pudding 126
Stilton twisted straws 158–9
stout: beef & ale pies, mash & liquor 186–7
strawberries
  berry crème tarts 98
  hidden clove, apple & strawberry strudel 139–40
  triple-layer berry Victoria sponge 31–2
strudel, hidden clove, apple & strawberry 139–40
sultanas
  carrot cake 38–9
  Cointreau & orange hot cross buns 226–7
  Nan's boiled fruit cake 41
  port-soaked Christmas cake 52–3
  spiced sultana bagels 240–1
sun-dried tomatoes: Mediterranean soda bread 214
swede and carrot mash with cumin 172–3

sweet potatoes
  cheese & onion pie 202–3
  chorizo, pepper & sweet potato tart 195
  chunky shepherd's pie 191–2
  fish pie 198
  roasted red pepper, squash & sweet potato soup 184

T
tarts
  berry crème tarts 98
  cherry Amaretto Bakewell tart 93
  chorizo, pepper & sweet potato tart 195
  cornflake tart 97
  pear & fig tarte tatin 110–11
  salmon, prawn & asparagus tart 204
the 3 P's roulade 141
toad in the hole, venison sausage & red onion 163
toffee
  sticky toffee pudding 126
  toffee apple crumble 120
tomatoes
  Mediterranean soda bread 214
  vegetable quiche 190
tottie scones 211
treacle: date & ginger cake 37
triple-layer berry Victoria sponge 31–2

V
vanilla custard 121
vegetables
  vegetable quiche 190
  see also carrots; potatoes etc
venison sausage & red onion toad in the hole 163
Victoria sponge, triple-layer berry 31–2

W
waffles
  cheese & ham waffles 207
  chocolate & banana waffles 146
walnuts
  apple, walnut & cinnamon buns 230–1
  mocha chocolate cake 30
  Nan's boiled fruit cake 41
  Nan's butterscotch brownies 68

Y
Yorkshire puddings, one-cup sage and onion 178

Conversion charts

Weight

¼ oz	7 g	8 oz (½ lb)	230 g	15¾ oz	450 g
½ oz	15 g	8¼ oz	235 g	1 lb [16 oz]	455 g
¾ oz	20 g	8½ oz	240 g	1¼ lb	570 g
1 oz	30 g	8¾ oz	250 g	1½ lb	680 g
1¼ oz	35 g	9 oz	255 g	1¾ lb	800 g
1½ oz	40 g	9¼ oz	260 g	2 lb	910 g
1¾ oz	50 g	9½ oz	270 g	2½ lb	1.2 kg
2 oz	55 g	9¾ oz	275 g	3 lb	1.4 kg
2¼ oz	65 g	10 oz	280 g	3½ lb	1.6 kg
2½ oz	70 g	10¼ oz	290 g	4 lb	1.8 kg
2¾ oz	75 g	10½ oz	300 g	4½ lb	2 kg
3 oz	85 g	10¾ oz	305 g	5 lb	2.3 kg
3¼ oz	90 g	11 oz	310 g	5½ lb	2.5 kg
3½ oz	100 g	11¼ oz	320 g	6 lb	2.7 kg
3¾ oz	105 g	11½ oz	325 g	6½ lb	3 kg
4 oz	115 g	11¾ oz	335 g	7 lb	3.2 kg
4¼ oz	120 g	12 oz	340 g	7½ lb	3.4 kg
4½ oz	130 g	12¼ oz	350 g	8 lb	3.6 kg
4¾ oz	135 g	12½ oz	355 g	8½ lb	3.8 kg
5 oz	140 g	12¾ oz	360 g	9 lb	4 kg
5¼ oz	150 g	13 oz	370 g	9½ lb	4.3 kg
5½ oz	155 g	13¼ oz	375 g	10 lb	4.5 kg
5¾ oz	160 g	13½ oz	385 g		
6 oz	170 g	13¾ oz	390 g		
6¼ oz	175 g	14 oz	400 g		
6½ oz	185 g	14¼ oz	405 g		
6¾ oz	190 g	14½ oz	415 g		
7 oz	200 g	14¾ oz	420 g		
7¼ oz	210 g	15 oz	430 g		
7½ oz	215 g	15¼ oz	435 g		
7¾ oz	220 g	15½ oz	445 g		

Volume

American	Metric	Fluid ounces
¼ tsp	1.25 ml	–
½ tsp	2.5 ml	–
1 tsp	5 ml	–
½ tbsp (1½ tsp)	7.5 ml	–
1 tbsp (3 tsp)	15 ml	–
2 tbsp	30 ml	1 fl oz
2½ tbsp	37.5 ml	1¼ fl oz
3 tbsp	45 ml	1½ fl oz
3½ tbsp	52.5 ml	1¾ fl oz
¼ cup (4 tbsp)	60 ml	2 fl oz
⅓ cup (5 tbsp)	80 ml	2½ fl oz
⅜ cup (6 tbsp)	90 ml	3 fl oz
½ cup (8 tbsp)	120 ml	4 fl oz
⅝ cup (10 tbsp)	150 ml	5 fl oz
⅔ cup (11 tbsp)	160 ml	5½ fl oz
¾ cup (12 tbsp)	180 ml	6 fl oz
⅞ cup (14 tbsp)	210 ml	7 fl oz
1 cup (16 tbsp)	240 ml	8 fl oz
1¼ cups	300 ml	10 fl oz
1⅓ cups	320 ml	10½ fl oz
1⅜ cups	330 ml	11 fl oz
1½ cups	360 ml	12 fl oz
1⅝ cups	390 ml	13 fl oz
1⅔ cups	400 ml	13½ fl oz
1¾ cups	420 ml	14 fl oz
2 cups (1 pt)	480 ml	16 fl oz
2½ cups	600 ml	20 fl oz
3 cups	720 ml	24 fl oz
3½ cups	840 ml	28 fl oz
4 cups (1 qt)	960 ml	32 fl oz

American	Metric
4½ cups	1 L
5 cups	1.2 L
5½ cups	1.3 L
6 cups	1.4 L
6½ cups	1.5 L
7 cups	1.7 L
7½ cups	1.8 L
8 cups (2 qt)	2 L
3 quarts	2.8 L
4 quarts (1 gl)	3.8 L
5 quarts	4.7 L
6 quarts	5.7 L
7 quarts	6.6 L
8 quarts	7.5 L

I am more thankful than I can ever express, for the opportunity to be able to write my own book. Thank you, reader, for believing in me enough to go out and buy it. Massive thanks go out to my incredible family and friends (you know who you are) but special mentions go to:

Nan and Grandad – I owe you my devotion to baking. Grandad, your love of cake carries on through me, and Nan – the apple of my eye, the most modest, kind woman to grace this Earth – you taught me everything I know and I hope I make you proud. I miss you every single day. Nan, Ivy – thank you for showing me that a diet of 95 per cent sugar can lead to a long and happy life; sweet dreams. Mam and Dad – thank you for your love and support; Mam, for teaching me the importance of always overdressing and never leaving home without lipstick. Letting me in on your trade kitchen secrets has shown me how to cater for and please the most demanding customers (mentioning no names, Benj!); Dad, thank you for just being you and being my Pop. Talking all things football and rugby has been a welcome distraction – you are my hero. Tanya and Ben, my big sis and little bro – I know you always have my back. Tanya, thank you for playing it cool. Ben, thanks for your advice, especially on the cheese-on-crumpets recipe - sadly, it didn't make the cut!

My girls (Wolfpack, Wednesday and School) – you've stuck by me and not batted an eyelid when I've cancelled plans or not replied to messages. I'm so grateful for your friendship – I owe you a lot more cake! Thank you for being my cheerleaders.

Anna – Blondie to my Brownie! You've always been by my side, we are like two peas in a pod. Thank you for never ever doubting me.

Beth and John – thank you for making me feel so welcome and letting me cover your kitchen in flour, icing sugar and everything else baking related. I am very lucky to have such a lovely, supportive second family.

The Great British Bake Off – thank you to everyone involved and Love Productions, from casting and production to directors, home economists and runners. And Mary, Paul, Mel and Sue: I have learnt so much and you allowed me to be me – that means more than you will ever know. And thanks to my eleven new friends – the Bakers of 2016: Jane, Andrew, Selasi, Benji, Rav, Tom, Val, Kate, Michael, Lou and Lee – who I regularly call on for advice or just have a good giggle with! Thank you lovely Shelagh and Amanda for holding my hand throughout everything.

Everyone at Ashlyn's, especially James and Elly – you helped me pursue my dream and encouraged me to take this opportunity and run with it.

Geraldine, Kate and Anna at Yellow Poppy – thank you for your belief in me from the very beginning and continual support. You took a chance on me and that means so much.

Thank you to Ebury who gave me this opportunity to write my first book, to Laura Higginson and Laura Nickoll for all you have put into it and for your patience: Laura N – my 2am emails were not ideal but you never huffed and puffed! And thanks to Louise for the stunning design.

Lou – you made my recipes look better than I ever could. You are so talented and the bakes are just beautiful. And thank you, Hannah, for sourcing wonderful props. Ellis – you have taken some of the most stunning photographs of my food I have ever seen! You 'get' me and my oddities and this is reflected in your pictures so beautifully. Thank you for the giggles and for not telling me off too much for chipped nails and hand burns!

Finally, my two boys – my Scottish one and my Pug one: Liam and Dennis. Thank you, Liam, for being there from the start. You encouraged me, picking me up and dusting me down when things went wrong and being the first to say 'see, I told you' when things went well. Thank you for putting up with me – I love you with all I have.

CB xxx

10 9 8 7 6 5 4 3 2 1

Ebury Press, an imprint of Ebury Publishing,
20 Vauxhall Bridge Road,
London, SW1V 2SA

Ebury Press is part of the Penguin Random House group
of companies whose addresses can be found at global.
penguinrandomhouse.com

Penguin
Random House
UK

First published by Ebury Press in 2017

www.penguin.co.uk

A CIP catalogue record for this book is available from
the British Library

Photography: Ellis Parrinder
Design: Louise Evans
Project management: Laura Nickoll
Food styling: Lou Kenney
Props styling: Hannah Wilkinson

ISBN: 9781785037078

Printed and bound in Italy by LEGO S.p.A.

Penguin Random House is committed to a sustainable
future for our business, our readers and our planet.
This book is made from Forest Stewardship Council®
certified paper.